WHEN THE RAIN STOPS

A MEMOIR

CORA WILTSHIRE

ISBN 979-8-89112-798-2 (Paperback)
ISBN 979-8-89112-799-9 (Digital)

Covenant Books
11661 Hwy 707
Murrells Inlet, SC 29576
www.covenantbooks.com

I love the Lord, for He heard my cries, and pitied every groan;
long as I live when troubles rise, I'll hasten to His throne.

—Psalm 116:1

CHAPTER 1

Weeping may endureth for a night, but joy cometh in the morning.
—Psalm 30:5

April 1966

It's going to rain later. It shouldn't matter, but somehow, it's the only thing that does. I wish it was a month from now. That's the mantra inside my seventeen-year-old brain. Over and over and over. For some reason that I don't even understand, I think in a month I'll be able to deal with this loss, this emptiness, this fear.

My father's funeral will start in an hour. I'm already dressed. My sisters need help with their hair. I can't help them. All I can think about is the rain that will fall on my father's face as he rests in the cold, dark grave. But I don't cry. Maybe that'll come later with the rain.

It seems to take forever, but finally I hear my mother's voice saying it's time to go.

Time for me to let go.

CHAPTER 2

Thy preparest a table before me in the presence of mine enemies.
—Psalm 23:5

1998

"Gentlemen, hear me well. Let yesterday be the last day you fail to complete your assignments and get them to me on time."

This is a conversation that's very straightforward and long overdue even though versions of it have been had before. I'm a five-foot-two-inch Black woman managing all white men—everyone so much taller than me. For me, all of that is immaterial. They have a job to do. And so do I.

I'm a senior executive in the homebuilding industry now, having gone through the ranks to get to this place in my career. But I still ask myself, "What on earth am I doing here?" Female and Black in a good ol' boy's world.

Gaining their respect wasn't easy, but it wasn't as difficult as it could have been. I've done each of their jobs before, and they know it. They understand that I understand what each of their jobs entail, so no excuses will work. Not now. Not ever.

My job is to understand the mission, communicate the mission to my team, and execute the mission together. Every time. They've been trained, but we can get better. Our customers depend on it. They depend on us. We won't let them down.

*****

I started out in human resources, recruiting and hiring for all positions including construction, sales, land, administration, and warranty service for the states of Texas and Louisiana. Growing my career in this industry led me into the world of selling new homes where, based on my performance, I was quickly promoted to the position of vice president of sales and marketing. In that role, I was responsible for selling homes as well as managing other sales professionals. Helping customers find their first or their forever home became more important to me than I ever imagined. Their excitement was contagious as they started on their new journey.

Perhaps that's the reason that ensuring excellent customer service became the driving force of my career. I understood that whatever was important to me as the leader was what would become important to those who had to do the hard work every day.

And I knew that the pride my team and I felt when we closed the door on our final product would be the same level of pride our customers would feel when they opened that door to their new home. They trusted us—with their dreams and their treasure.

I never took their trust for granted. And I believed it needed to be earned.

Every day.

CHAPTER 3

Now faith is the substance of things hoped
for, the evidence of things not seen.

—Hebrews 11:1

2000

So my mother has cancer. There is no cure. For a control freak like me, this is the most horrific, excruciating news ever. I can't fix it. And I don't know how to be who I am without her. But I must learn.

*****

Walking down the sterile, antiseptic-smelling hallway in the hospital, I hear my footsteps. I dread why I'm here—to visit my mother on my lunch hour. Maybe I should have eaten something first. Maybe that's why my stomach feels so unsettled. But I know better.

It's time. Before I enter, I pause at her door to look through the narrow glass window. How is it possible that this "giant" of a woman can seem so small, so fragile? She's surrounded by blips and beeps, wires and hanging bags.

Alone with her in that cold hospital room with my favorite scarf wrapping her now balding head, I ask her, "Mama, are you scared?"

In that silent moment, I remember how I felt in high school when I was the only one who knew the answer to a tough question. Well, that's how I feel now about what I am sure will be my mother's answer. I am certain, confident. I'm waiting to hear, "No, sweetheart, I am not afraid." Those words will let me breathe. Let me believe in miracles.

Faith. My mother was a woman of absolute and unshakable faith. It sustained her, surrounded her, lifted her up. One of her favorite sayings was, "Through faith all things are possible." I believed it too. I believed her.

Then I hear my mother's response. Unfortunately, her answer mirrors my own. We are both afraid. But there is a calm resolve in her eyes that I cannot match. Even though she feels the fear, she does not fear the feeling. She embraces it. Her unwavering faith lets her know where her journey will end. And she's ready to receive her heavenly rewards for a life well lived.

Because of her strength in that room, in that moment, there is a quiet acceptance. We both feel it in the sad smile we share.

*****

My time with her is over for now. Time to go back to the "real" world of meetings, conference calls, and reports, where no one knows my heart is breaking with every breath I take. A world where everything has changed and nothing else matters. But I must keep going. My mother would expect nothing less.

And I will not let her down.

CHAPTER 4

*Honour thy Father and thy Mother: that thy days may
be long upon the land which the Lord giveth thee.*

—Exodus 20:12

January 1966

My father was a Southern Baptist minister. He was also a strict disciplinarian. In my father's eyes, the two were inexorably linked. His beliefs were strongly held and unyielding, informed by the teachings in the Bible.

He demanded obedience and excellence—constantly reminding me and my siblings that "if you're not going to do something right, then don't do it at all." Of course, we never had the option of *not* doing it.

His presence loomed large. I thought my father was six feet tall until my mother told me, after his death from an aneurysm, that he was only five feet, six inches. Somehow, he remains six feet tall to me.

*****

Aneurysm. Can that really be a word? Unfortunately, yes, and it described my father's condition. That strong, hardworking, never-missed-a-day-of-work man was struck down at forty-one years old. Back then, the doctors explained it as a blood bubble on his brain that had burst. They needed to operate immediately. My mother and I were the only ones at the hospital, and a decision had to be made. Operate and risk death on the table. Don't operate and ensure immediate death. No decision really.

He survived the operation, but it left him paralyzed on his right side. He couldn't walk or talk coherently and needed around-the-clock care. Because we are Black, he was put in the "colored" ward of the county hospital where there were no provisions for around-the-clock care. So that duty fell to my mother and me.

*****

At seventeen, I was the oldest at home with five younger siblings relying on me. I knew how to drive, but we didn't have a car that worked. Thank God for true friends. My best friend would drive me to my father's job to pick up his weekly disability check of thirty-five dollars. She would then take me to the local grocery store to try to find something to feed my siblings for the week. Mostly canned goods and the cheapest cuts of meat.

Sunday nights through Fridays, I was in charge: combing hair, washing clothes, making lunches and dinners, paying bills, and helping with homework. The youngest was only six, so at least no homework for him. Also, checking doors and windows twice before I could go to bed.

My mother would stay at the hospital looking after my father's care Sunday nights to Friday evenings. One of her brothers would pick her up and bring her home. Those Fridays were so special to all of us—we missed her, and she missed us. Every Friday, I tried to cook the best meal I could. I wanted a hot meal for her—the first one of her week. I couldn't stay to enjoy dinner with her. There was only time for a quick hug. It's time for my shift.

Before my mother arrived, I gathered my books and other odds and ends to take to the hospital to spend the weekend. The nurses had shown my mother and me what needed to be done and how often.

It was hard to rest sitting up in a chair all night. I knew. And once again, it was my turn to sit in that chair. I wouldn't sleep, though. There was no sleeping through all the hospital noises any-way—the chirping EKGs, the intercom calls just frequent enough to keep my shoulders raised too high to sleep deeply, and the less frequent, but heartrending sounds of other patients in pain. And there was always the fear of drifting off and not being there when my father might need me.

But sleep didn't really matter anyway. I've got homework to do, and I only had a little while before my father would need me again. I'd leave Sunday night when my mother returned. I'd sleep once I was home, after I checked the doors and windows. Twice.

CHAPTER 5

Keep your heart with all vigilance, for from it flow the springs of life.
—Proverbs 4:23

January 1966

The winter dance is coming up. I won't be able to go. There are more important things to do. I'm still sad, but I can't show it. That would disrespect both my mother and my father. I don't have a dress anyway. Or a date.

For just a moment, though, I close my eyes; and I am there. Soft lights, colorful balloons, and crepe paper streamers have transformed the old, sweaty socks–smelling gym into a magical place. I hear the music coming from a tape recording. I see the flowing, kaleidoscopic colors of dresses, and girls giggling in self-conscious clusters. I look down. I can see my dress, and I love it. It is robin's-egg blue—my favorite color. My date is tall and handsome, and he has given me a corsage—one small, perfect calla lily, which I will keep pressed in my geometry book. Forever.

*****

I open my eyes and immediately feel the guilt of wanting. I'm back where I belong. It was just a wish. A dream that can't come true.

*****

My father is coming home today. He's in a wheelchair, and his doctors have told us he will never walk again. He still needs all the help my mother and I provided while he was in the hospital. At least my mother and I don't have to sleep sitting in a chair.

This proud man has worked hard his entire life: his eight-to-five construction job during the week, frying burgers in a diner at night, and mowing lawns in the rich neighborhoods with my two older brothers on the weekends.

But now, because he's no longer in the hospital, the disability checks disappear. We must go on welfare. Not for money so much as for food. Milk and eggs that are dried, a block of neon-yellow cheese that comes in a cardboard box, bologna that comes in a plastic tube needing to be sliced, and a congealed meat product that comes in a can without a label. But we're grateful even though it's humiliating.

*****

We're here. At the welfare office—this place that smells of fear, sweat, and desperation. Am I going to smell like that when I leave? That thought scares me more than the reason we're here. Finally, it's our turn to make our case to the welfare lady. She is a middle-aged woman whose expression says it all: she looks as though she's been dumped in a foreign place to do a job she despises. It's impossible to know if she despises her job or just the people who benefit from her work. Perhaps it's both. My father hands her the already filled out paperwork. We're prepared. Her review is perfunctory; she's seen all these documents before, and she is not moved by our circumstances. She asks a few meaningless questions that are already answered in the paperwork, which she won't bother to read. Finally, she applies the "Approved" rubber stamp.

My father thanks her. She does not respond. He tells her their help will be temporary. He tells her he will be back, walking upright, to cancel their help one day soon. It's easy to see that the welfare lady clearly doesn't believe him. She doesn't say a word. She doesn't even attempt to mask her disdain.

*****

How can a place feel cold and hot at the same time? As we make our way out through that oversized, depressing space where so many others like us—who look like us—wait their turn to hope for help, feeling completely helpless, I feel defeated, somehow not worthy. As I prepare the wheelchair to leave, my father sees my face and recognizes my shame. "Lift your head up, Cora. Don't ever let anybody shake your faith or your pride." I look down at my father as I push him toward the exit. I'm dumbfounded, but thankfully, he can't see my face.

Faith? Pride? Those words don't belong here! They clang like the vilest of obscenities in this horrible place of fear and hopelessness. But I choose to believe my father. It's the only way I can make it outside to the cleansing sunshine.

Another fear sweeps through me as we go through the doors onto the sidewalk. I realize that my nose has gotten used to the depressing smell of that place that even God seems to have forsaken.

*****

My father continued to prove that he was a hardworking, determined man. It took some time and a lot of tenacity and painfully excruciating work, but within just a few months, he left his wheelchair behind and "walked" on two wooden crutches borrowed from a neighbor into the welfare office and cancelled their help. We met with the same disdainful welfare lady. When she saw my father standing before her with his cancellation paperwork, there was only one word for her expression: disbelief. Somewhat reluctantly, she thanked my father.

*****

It was late April when my father died. Four and a half months after that surgery and all of those long nights of sleeplessness and worry. Every important milestone awaiting me would happen without him. My high school graduation in just a few weeks and going to college as the first person in my family to do so. I would miss his pride. My career in construction, which was itself a tribute to him. I would miss his slight nod and quick smile that signaled his silent approval. My marriage to an honorable man he would never meet. I would miss holding his arm as I walked down the aisle toward that man. The birth of my children. I would miss his counsel.

*****

But now, looking back through the veil of lived experiences and understanding, I realize that my father was always there. He never left. Even though I couldn't see him, I could feel his presence once I allowed myself to accept his absence.

*****

He didn't have much to leave us. Just an example to follow. And that was enough. It was everything.

CHAPTER 6

For everything there is a season. A time for every
activity under heaven. A time to be born and a time
to die. A time to plant and a time to harvest.

—Ecclesiastes 3:1–2

August 2001

I never thought of my sons as pallbearers. Today they are being inducted into a heartbreaking, solemn brotherhood. It is not their choice. It is, though, their sacred duty and their honor. They must carry their beloved grandmother to her final resting place. I know they fear this overwhelmingly daunting task, so now is not the time to allow myself to hurt like a daughter who has lost her mother. I must be strong for my sons.

*****

Grief. Even the word sounds heavy. It lies like a stone next to your heart and robs you of rest and respite. Of smiles and happiness. The look on everyone's faces mirrors how I feel. Does my face look like that? There's been pain before in my life but none greater than that of losing my mother.

Before we go to the church to start this already painful day, we gather as a family in the house where my mother lived and died. We gather to pray, to comfort each other.

As a tribute to my mother, my sisters and I are all dressed in the same color—a soft cream. To us, it speaks to who our mother was: a strong, fearless woman who possessed a gentleness of spirit that felt pure and untouched by the stains of this world.

At the church, we line up by age with the oldest going in first. I fall right in the middle, and I feel the support of my family in front of me and those behind. It doesn't really seem to make a difference, though. No one wants to be here, and there's no comfort anywhere. The church is overflowing with mourners. I barely notice them. Walking slowly up the aisle to the casket where my mother lay, I focused on the program in my hand that I don't remember being given. It's finally my turn to stand before that casket. My husband tries to comfort me. I don't want that. I need to feel this. I need to feel everything.

My mother is so small now. There's a slight smile on her lips as though she's already resting comfortably in the arms of her Lord. She looks beautiful. She's dressed like her daughters. We are one together, and we're each completely alone.

*****

It's time to say a final goodbye to the one person who knows me best. Who understands me without words. My mother fought her painful, soul-crushing battle with cancer for a heroic ten months—from October to August. She had one request of God: to let her live long enough to see my youngest son graduate from college. My son graduated from university in May. Mama died in August. She was too ill to travel, but she was still there—cheering, crying, and praising God. We felt her presence.

*****

Her journey here has now ended. Her mission is accomplished. She's now with the Lord she worshipped reverently. She's no longer in pain; she no longer needs to worry about how the family she left behind will cope. She cherished all of her children and grandchildren of which there are many. And she taught us well. We will survive—just a little less whole.

What greater privilege than to have her grandsons bear her in her casket on her final earthly journey? How difficult a task it must be for them, feeling her weight shift slightly with each measured step. They know how important this job is. I can tell their burden is a heavy one by the strained shoulders, furrowed brows, and determined faces. I know their pain is both physically and emotionally wrenching. Which is worse? We know. Theirs is a shared responsibility that they will forever remember even though their hearts will never be the same—a piece forever missing. They loved her. She treasured them.

*****

We buried my mother on a Sunday. Monday was a workday. No time to reflect, no time to properly grieve, no desire to stay in that terrible space of mourning, no strength to escape from it. It must have been a week or so later, still in that sluggish morass of grief and emptiness, that I felt an overwhelming desire to be with my mother. It was late, or early, depending on your sensibilities, when I got out of bed and went into my closet. I laid out a black pantsuit, my best cream-colored silk blouse, and black pumps. I wrote a note to my husband instructing him that those laid-out clothes were meant to be my burial clothes. I was absolutely convinced; I was completely certain that once I laid my head back on my pillow, I would drift off into that vast void to be joined forever with my mother, father, and little brother who had all gone before. Who were waiting for me.

I said my prayers and asked God for special blessings and protection for those I would leave behind. I would still watch over them—just not from here. I felt the need to go. I needed this unbearable pain to go away.

I didn't expect to wake up the next day. When I woke up that morning—early enough to retrieve the note to my husband that he never knew existed—I realized that my time had not yet come. There was more work for me to do. I still needed to carry out my mother's wishes for me to succeed. I still needed to be here for my family.

Suddenly, I felt a lightness of spirit, a sense of something like joyfulness unlike anything I had experienced before or since. It felt like a state of grace, and I was grateful. I rehung my clothes in their proper place, put my shoes away. Time to start a new day. A new chapter.

*****

When I think back to that evening, I had believed it was just my heart that was broken. I realized in the early morning light that it was I who was broken. Unable—or maybe unwilling—to cope. I prayed then. A prayer giving thanks to the same God I'd been praying to my entire life, for saving me. And forgiving myself for not being able to save my mother. I think for the first time in my life, I understood the strength of unconditional love and the real power of prayer.

Memories. One day they will take the place of this overwhelming grief. Small flashes of half-forgotten stories that can be recalled to dull the loneliness and pain, allowing for soft smiles that can be shared.

I'm an orphan now. I am thankful for angels.

CHAPTER 7

Peace I leave with you, my peace I give unto you:
not as the world giveth, give I unto you.

—John 14:27

1976

It was the bicentennial. It felt like the whole country was celebrating. My mother's church organized a bus tour of some of the original thirteen colonies. I lived in Connecticut then, and my mother was able to visit for a short time.

My second to youngest brother died that year while my mother was on that trip. He was nineteen years old. He was only four days into his brand-new college career. He had gotten there on his own merit through a football scholarship that promised to pay for everything. I remember being so proud of him. I was excited for the new experiences awaiting him—that mind-numbing but exhilarating feeling of being on your own, of starting something you've been dreaming about since peewee football days. He promised my mother that he would buy her a new house if he was talented enough to make it to the pros. I believed he was that talented. We all did—especially my mother.

*****

Unfortunately, God had other plans. It was August in Texas, and the football team was working out under that hot, unrelenting summer sun. While running drills, my brother collapsed and was taken to the local state hospital for what everyone thought was just heat exhaustion. No one knew about the enlarged heart condition that would take his life later that same day. No doctors checked on him. The nurses monitored his progress periodically. Hospital records showed that no one checked on him after visiting hours ended at 8:00 p.m. when his visiting coaches left. He died at 8:30 p.m., completely alone.

The news of my brother's grossly untimely death was delivered to my husband, whose difficult task it was to tell me. I was at work. My manager, who had been briefed by my husband, came to my desk and quietly told me it was time for me to go home early. No reason was given, and oddly, I didn't ask for one. There was something about her demeanor that seemed to demand urgency. She told me my husband was already waiting for me downstairs.

When you are a mother, your first thought is something horrific has happened to your child. I could barely get my belongings together fast enough to leave. The elevator seemed to take hours to travel down four floors. As the doors opened, my first sight was of my small son crawling by his dad's feet. I remember smiling with an exhalation of relief. I remember saying—or maybe I just thought it—"Well, that's one fear allayed."

As I picked up my one-year-old, I saw my husband's face. There was only one question I needed answered, and I wouldn't—couldn't wait to get to the car. "What's happened?"

I remember hearing the words: "I'm so sorry, but your brother has died." *What!* Which one? How? When? So many questions. No sufficient answers. My thoughts immediately turned to my mother who wouldn't get this heart-wrenching, unbearable news immediately. She was still on her bus tour, and it would take two more days for my mother to return home. It took me and my husband two hours less than that to get to her house. I was there when she arrived but stayed out of sight until she could be told her world was never going to be the same again. Her child was gone.

All of her children that she expected to see were there waiting for her in the yard. She thought everyone was there to welcome her home. She was smiling and happy. Until. My oldest brother walked her into her house, into her bedroom. Everyone slowly followed them inside. I knew—we all knew—the exact moment my mother heard those unspeakable words that had to be spoken. Her son, her promise for a better future, was gone. I will never be able to unhear, or forget, that long, anguished, wailing moan that was my mother's grief overflowing. Enveloping her. Rendering her speechless, motionless.

I went to her then. A hug was all I had to give. Maybe that's all that was needed in that moment.

*****

After the funeral, I stayed with my mother for a few days. It's an interesting phenomenon; before the funeral, the house is overflowing with people, and you just want to be alone. After the funeral, the house is too quiet, and all you want is a distraction. That's why I stayed. To be silent when she needed it and to be a distraction when she wanted one.

*****

Finally, it was Sunday. I was flying back home the next day. Because my mother never missed a Sunday service, I got dressed for church assuming she was doing the same. When I saw her, though, she was still in her bathrobe. I was shocked. This woman of faith never missed church—even when she wasn't feeling her best. She always went. I asked her if she needed help getting dressed. She told me she couldn't go back to that church. She said it in that tone that meant, "Don't try to change my mind." I didn't understand the "why" because she didn't give me a reason.

Well, I am my mother's daughter and *not* talking was not an option. As gently as I could, I asked her why she couldn't go back to church. Her answer was as straightforward as it was heartbreaking.

She said, "If I go back, all I'll be able to see is my son's casket resting in front of the pulpit, and I can't bear it."

In that quiet, still house, I understood. I also knew if my mother didn't go back to church that very Sunday, she would lose her center, her true north, the one thing that tethered her to this world where she'd already suffered so much loss. I also realized she wasn't able to say my brother's name. It hurt too much. My mother loved all her children, but this son was somehow "more." We all felt it, knew it, understood it. Accepted it.

I promised her I would be with her every step of the way, but we were going to church. We would sit in the last pew if she wanted. We would leave whenever she wanted, but we needed to go. She made it all the way through the service sitting next to me in the last pew. True to her feeling of devastation of that loss, though, I never heard my mother say my brother's name again.

*****

My youngest son was born a couple of years later. In tribute to my brother—and, hopefully, as a gift to my mother—I named my son after my brother. This new baby would free my mother to be able to say his name without sorrow, but with joy. I remember my mother always saying that she hoped God would let her live long enough to see my youngest son graduate from college.

It's taken me years, but I realize now why my mother's greatest wish and her last answered prayer was that God would let her live to see my youngest son graduate from college. It's because *her* son of the same name couldn't.

*****

We had buried my brother without knowing why he died. The not knowing made an already unbearable situation so much worse. Nothing made sense.

I remember how difficult it was to get accurate information from the local coroner, then later the state coroner's office. Every blank on the death certificate was filled out with these words: Sickle Cell Anemia. We were poor, but the one thing my mother made sure of was that we got physical exams every year from the public clinic. So we all knew my brother did not have sickle cell anemia. It was hard to get even something like paperwork right when you're Black and poor in the South.

My mother had to sue the state to force them to give us the real reason for his death. Can you imagine burying your young, strong, athletic son without knowing what brought you to that place? It's inhumane for no good reason. Just the fear of lawsuits from a distraught parent. My mother had to sue the state to get information rightfully owed her about how her son had died and the circumstances surrounding his death. She didn't sue for money. She only asked for the reason her son was dead.

Between the death of the attending physician, a fire in the hospital that apparently destroyed all records relating to that time, and a general reluctance to admit neglectful treatment of my brother, it took ten years to finally learn the truth. Ten years! My brother died from an undetected, hence undiagnosed, enlarged heart.

Finally, answers.

CHAPTER 8

Therefore whoever heareth these sayings of mine, and doeth them, I will liken him unto a wise man, which built his house upon a rock.
—Matthew 7:24

1976

Seeing the devastating toll my brother's death had on my mother, I made the decision to move back to Texas to be with my family. My husband, small son, and I would start over in this place I thought never to return. My return meant finding a new job. The recruiter I consulted brought me into the world of new homebuilding—merely a job of opportunity at the time. Finding work in that industry was a fluke, a being-in-the-right-place-at-the-right-time kind of thing. I knew nothing about that business—I simply needed a new job because my family needed me again. Surprisingly, it would become my life's work. My career.

I interviewed for, and was offered, the position of director of human resources. In that role, it was my job to recruit, interview, and hire talented individuals for every position in the company, from administration to sales and construction management.

Thankfully, there were already job descriptions in place for each position. Those documents would inform my interview questions and fine-tune my ability to select the right candidates for the right positions. I'm a believer that God gives each of us at least one talent. And mine, turns out, is the ability to quickly assess and identify people's strengths and weaknesses. It allows me to recognize and hire truly gifted and talented people. I was proud of their successes. They were my contributions to my company's success.

*****

Getting hired by that company wasn't simple or easy. Just as there were already job descriptions in place, there was also a set of prerequisites that every candidate had to meet. There were four in all. If even one requirement wasn't up to the company's already established standards, that candidate would not be considered for employment. Those criteria were objective ones, easily quantifiable, making the process easy for candidates to understand and the results more acceptable.

A successful candidate would first have to pass a written test consisting of mathematical questions, calculations, and equations. Once that hurdle was cleared, they were administered a three-hundred-question personality test—specifically designed by outside professionals to determine whether the candidate's overall temperament and work ethic aligned with the goals and objectives of the company. In other words, would they be a good fit?

Third, the candidate was sent to a psychologist who would administer the Wexler Adult Intelligence Scale (WAIS), better known as an IQ test. The lowest acceptable IQ for a management position, which included every position except administration and sales, was 120—a hefty twenty points above average at the time. Clearly, only the best and brightest need apply.

Fourth and last, the successful candidate could not have applied for, or received, unemployment insurance at any time. The rationale behind this requirement was simple: industrious, hardworking people would always be able to find employment even if it wasn't ultimately where they wanted to be.

That template worked exceedingly well. It brought highly competent, intelligent, and driven individuals into the company. Individuals who would make great general managers who just happened to be in the homebuilding industry rather than only being good construction managers. Success followed. For the company and its employees.

*****

Initially, the company focused solely on building communities with single-family homes with large yards. It was Texas, after all, and land was plentiful. All new homebuilders vied for the same customer base—families who wanted all brick homes with fenced backyards where children could safely play.

Our company was led by a true entrepreneur. He had vision. He saw a new, emerging market in which singles and newly married couples without children would prefer a more urban setting without the accompanying headaches and expense of home maintenance. He envisioned a new frontier: condominiums. Virtually unheard of at that time, in that place.

And it became my job to fill the sales position for that new vision. Not surprisingly, literally no experienced sales professional wanted to take a chance in this new arena. In an uncomfortable conversation with my manager, the president of the company, I had to deliver the news that I was unable to find a suitable candidate. Then something happened that took me completely by surprise. My boss said to me, "You know, Cora, I've been looking at *your* personality test, and you are a good match for a sales position." To say that I was dumbfounded is a complete understatement. I'd never sold anything in my life and didn't want to start now. What was he thinking? And how could I get out of there and keep my current job intact?

The good news was that he didn't try to pressure me. He knew I liked a challenge, and if I sat there long enough and mulled this insane idea over, I'd likely agree. He didn't speak. Finally, I said "Okay, I'll try it out, but if I don't like it—or more realistically—am no good at it, I will be able to return to my HR position." He promised to hold my current position open until I had a chance to try it out and hopefully, succeed at selling condos.

There's something to be said about fear being a great motivator. Because I was so sure I wouldn't sell anything to anyone, it became my mission to try to sell a condo to everyone I met. Who knew when I'd sell another one? I stayed in sales for fourteen months, during which I was the number one salesperson in the company starting from my very first month. I was promoted to vice president of sales in six months and set sales records that still stand to this day. I never returned to my HR position, but I never grew to enjoy that part of the business.

*****

Company policy at the time was that the track to become a senior manager would be from the construction side of the business, so I transitioned from sales. I started over, going from vice president of sales to the entry-level position of construction superintendent trainee. My income went from six figures to a very small five figures, and I couldn't have been happier. This more "hands-on" job suited me better; watching empty land turn into brand-new homes for families was rewarding and satisfying work.

*****

Building a career in this industry wasn't easy, but I didn't expect it to be. Actually, I didn't know what I expected. What I got was a bottoms-up education of how a house is put together, piece by piece. And I saw how those houses became homes for the families who had entrusted us with their dreams and hard-earned savings.

I learned that racial bias and misogyny are real and reside everywhere. It touched every aspect of my construction career—from having to stop wearing perfume and makeup to prevent unsavory comments from contractors, to wearing shirts buttoned high enough to ward off stolen peaks down my shirt while going over blueprints. I needed to stay focused on the task at hand, which was to manage the people and projects under my command rather than wasting time and energy warding off unwanted attention. There needed to be no ambiguity about our roles: mine was to lead; theirs was to follow my lead. No banter, no debate. No nonsense. Promotions came from that discipline and hard work, and I eventually became a member of the senior management team.

*****

I've always loved being "first." In everything. Who wouldn't? But in the construction industry, for me at this time, being first meant being alone. Alone to navigate literally every situation I found myself in because there was no historical data to read and draw from. There was no mentor for me. No trailblazer. No one to bounce ideas or issues off of who came from a point of view like mine. So I decided to do what I'd always been taught to do by my father—give my very best every time and steadily strive to get better. All my lessons had to be learned the hard way. One at a time.

Familiarity. What I would have given to see others who look like me in this vast sea of faces. This industry doesn't attract people of color; whether by a lack of interest and initiative or by design, I don't know. I remember being in a meeting where senior management was trying to understand why there was a dearth of minorities in the homebuilding industry—specifically in our company. At least they were willing to explore the question. I remember the uncomfortable feeling in the room, where I was the only minority and the only woman. A kind of self-conscious tension was palpable in even saying the necessary words out loud. It was clear they were afraid of saying the wrong thing. They didn't want to appear biased in any way, so they were afraid to ask the right questions, the tough questions.

I decided to take the initiative to make it "okay" to discuss this topic that was so delicate for them; tortuous for me. I finally said, "Gentlemen, as minorities, we know what to expect when the doors of corporate America open. We expect to see people who look like you, and that's okay. We just want the opportunity to walk through those doors. We'll deal with whatever comes next."

They all looked at me as though I was speaking a foreign language. They'd heard and understood the words but weren't quite sure how to take those words and turn them into meaningful actions. But at least, they felt freer to actually talk openly about what they feared would be a difficult discussion—finding a way forward to attract and retain diversity in our industry. Our company.

Unfettered now, the ideas started to flow. The meeting became a lively discourse with ideas that turned into action plans with assignments and time lines for the progress and results we sought. I ended up being the unofficial chair of that meeting. Essentially, I learned how to manage the process of managing: people, schedules, and expectations. I learned these things the same way I'd learned everything else in my life—one step at a time, giving my best effort every step of the way.

I am proud of my fellow managers who were willing to follow my lead on this sensitive topic that was important to all of us.

Especially to me.

CHAPTER 9

*For this my son was dead, and is alive again; he was
lost, and is found. And they began to be merry.*

—Luke 15:24

2001

I have three sons. I met my eldest son when he was old enough to
have a son of his own. I had wondered for so many years if that
meeting would ever happen. And then, if it did, how it would feel to
both of us. It's not that I didn't know where he was exactly; it's that I
wasn't allowed to know *him*.

*****

I was not my husband's first choice for a life partner, and he was
not mine. We both had to find each other when the time was right

for us to meet as soulmates. But out of my husband's first marriage came a wonderful gift—a son.

His mother and father—my husband now—realized that theirs wouldn't be a forever family. The biological mother received primary custody of that precious two-year-old. Because my husband wanted the best for both of them, he acceded to his ex-wife's request and allowed her and his son to relocate to another state so she could be close to her family and they could be there for them. That was what he believed would be best for his son.

When I came into my husband's life, he did not expect to be excluded from his son's life. He did not expect such a level of malevolence from his son's mother that she would purposely keep them apart. She made excuses that were gossamer thin. We pushed, demanded the agreement they had both signed be honored. She didn't care. I watched as my new husband quietly mourned the loss of that special attachment with his firstborn. I felt the weight of knowing I was the reason for that loss. And so, years passed with no contact between father and son. Many precious experiences and memories were missed.

*****

Family. I'm a product of a large, blended family. We didn't call it that when I was growing up. We were just brothers and sisters. But when we want to know from whence we came and from whom, nothing will prevent the finding out of that knowledge. This young man found us—found his dad and his brothers. He found me—his "other" mother waiting to embrace him and welcome him into the family that was already his.

And now I am about to meet him for the first time. He and his small family are visiting us, and he's waiting for me to get home from work. This is hard for me. The unexpected is uncomfortable. I'm not in control of how things will go. Can I hug him? Will he hug me? I wonder if this is hard for him too. So far, my knowledge of this son is in the form of a small, pocket-sized picture of a newborn that my husband has. That picture has always been tucked into the side of my dresser mirror. We see him every day, but we don't know the child he was or the man he has become.

I was grateful when he reached out to his brothers years ago—who always knew about him through stories from their shared dad. And now I'm about to meet my new son. Not one I birthed, but one given to me by God.

As if we have rehearsed this moment a thousand times, we walk toward each other. He's holding his infant son and the three of us embrace. We're both smiling those smiles that are reserved for moments when no words are spoken. They're not needed. Acceptance feels like forgiveness and grace.

*****

I am still amazed by the void this son now fills in our family—one I didn't even realize existed. His intellect and quick wit remind me of his dad and brothers. His wife's dedication to family and career reminds me of myself—or so I like to believe. And his children remind me that I am blessed beyond measure to be a grandmother. Yes, at that moment, I became a grandmother to the infant son of my eldest son.

I became Gram. The best title ever.

CHAPTER 10

Love is patient, love is kind. It does not envy, it does not boast, it is not proud. It is not rude, it is not self-seeking, it is not easily angered, it keeps no record of wrongs. Love does not delight in evil but rejoices with the truth.

—1 Corinthians 13:4–6

January 2012

It's too early for this. On my best day, I'm not an early riser. My husband knows this better than anyone, so why is he tapping my shoulder? I'm confused, still more asleep than awake. And truth be told, not happy about being awakened before I was ready. Why is he waking me up? What is he saying? I roll over to hear him better. He's saying that he's not feeling well and needs my help. I'm still not coherent enough to grasp the gravity of the situation. I'm still trying to understand why he's up so early. I finally understood enough to know that he must need me to help him somehow.

I sit up and ask what exactly it is that he's feeling. For some reason he seems unable to communicate effectively. He seems disoriented and confused. He looks forlorn. Now I'm beginning to feel concerned. My very intelligent and well-spoken husband who has never been at a loss for words now seems unsure or nervous about talking to me.

I had no idea that early morning that we were about to embark on a nearly three-year journey that would involve eighteen different specialists, brain surgery at the National Institutes of Health, five separate hospital stays, and a nursing home admission. I had no idea

31

that I would have to treat my sixty-four-year-old husband as though he was a toddler and take away his car keys. I had no idea.

I got up and got dressed. I was assuming he was doing the same, but he was not. He was just sitting there on the window seat in his closet waiting for me to tell him what to do. Now I'm worried. I told him that we were going to the Urgent Care facility located near our home. I got him clothes to put on. He was obeying as though he was a small child—just following directions.

In ten minutes, we were waiting to see the doctor. Her diagnosis was that he needed to see a specialist although she didn't appear to know what kind of specialist he needed. Her advice was that I call our primary care physician for more direction. I made that call while still sitting in the parking lot of that small strip center because I had no idea where his doctor would tell me to take him. That call began our journey to those eighteen different specialists—none of whom seemed to know exactly what was wrong. The only thing each of them seemed to know was theirs was not the specialty he needed. Next referral to the next specialist. Meanwhile, my husband's health kept declining.

There's too much I didn't know. I didn't know why my husband couldn't remember how to get home from the grocery store we'd been going to for years. I didn't know why our longtime family doctor no longer wanted to be his doctor. I later found out that it was because my normally mild-mannered husband lost his temper and yelled at her. I didn't even know why his temper was so short. Most of all, I didn't know how to help him because I didn't understand what was happening to him. To us. I didn't know what I didn't know, so what questions do I ask? All I did know was that I had to find out. Now.

With that realization, I embarked on one of the longest, most unsettling, and difficult journeys of my life. I was losing the man I married, the father of my children, my best friend. And I didn't know how to help him.

*****

Finally, twelve agonizing months and eighteen specialists later, a diagnosis from a newly minted doctor, an endocrinologist who wasn't afraid to ask probing questions. He performed a thorough examination including comparing the picture on my husband's driver's license to his current face. He assessed everything I told him without preexisting assumptions based on ethnicity, age, or bias. Probably the most important thing he did was the simplest thing of all. He listened. And he knew exactly what was wrong with my husband. Finally, a diagnosis.

Cushing's disease. A brain tumor. I'd never heard of this culprit that's taken over my husband. I didn't even know how to spell it. All I needed to know in that moment was that we would finally get the help my husband so desperately needed. I asked question after question. I took notes because I had to remember everything. I had to tell my sons. They would need to know there was a tumor on their dad's brain that was so small it looked like the end of a ballpoint pen. How can something so tiny cause so much pain and suffering? So much chaos and confusion?

Now the real journey began. It would be arduous and overwhelming. At times, I would feel completely alone without the determination to continue. But I must and I would. My family was my rock, and they surrounded me and helped me every step of the way. Except for those lonely moments in the middle of the night when I was alone. Prayer was where I turned then, and I was comforted. Until the next night.

*****

The operation took hours. My sons were there with me, waiting for news that everything went well. That the tumor was completely gone without lasting damage to its host: my husband, their father.

While we waited, the visitor's waiting room was almost always full with other families awaiting news of their loved ones. Doctors came and went, but not the one we were waiting for. Minutes turned into hours. The sun had set long ago. We still waited. The room was empty now except for our vigil.

Finally, the doctor appeared. By now, I was convinced I should be prepared to hear words I would dread. I was prepared to hear them but not show any emotion because I must be strong for my sons. Of course, my sons were thinking exactly the same thing about their reactions so they could be strong for me. I know how blessed I am to have these strong young men by my side. Not just in this moment, but always. Fortunately, the doctor delivered the best news that was possible at that moment. The entire tumor had been removed without the need to remove any part of my husband's pituitary gland. But recovery would be long and uneven. There would be more bad days than good ones. And there was no way to know what to expect. We could not prepare for the unknown. We must blindly follow the lead of my extremely ill husband who didn't know where he was going.

No one knew then that the recovery would take another eighteen months—with five different hospital stays, admission into a nursing home that smelled of loneliness and decay, in-home nurses, and therapists. So many decisions to make every day. More than thirteen different medications to administer five times a day, every day, and not knowing which of those medications would work and which wouldn't. Trial and error until the mix was correct. Or until something else needed to change.

Even though I was warned that my husband's healing process wouldn't be in a straight line, from extremely ill to completely healed, I didn't know—couldn't know—what that would entail. I expected the process to evolve through incremental steps that would build upon themselves one after the last, seeing small improvements every day until he was completely whole. But I was only guessing because no one could really know what "improvement" would look like or how long it would take. The doctor had warned us. And unfortunately, he was right. The actual journey toward healing neither looked nor felt anything like a straight line.

*****

Situational dementia. That was just one of his post-surgery diagnoses, which was determined once he was checked into the nursing home. That condition is the result of an illness so severe the patient's attitude and reactions mimic those of some patients with Alzheimer's—they don't recognize most of the people they've known for years, don't know they are being difficult and uncooperative, aren't aware of their surroundings. And in my husband's case, the enduring desire to be at home. Because of that urgent desire, one night my husband called 911 from the phone in his room. I'm still surprised he remembered the three-digit phone number since he remembered little else. He wanted the police to come, pick him up, and bring him home. He was convinced he had been kidnapped because the nurses refused to let him go home. I got the call from the 911 operator just after ten thirty that night confirming two things: first, that I was his primary caregiver and second, that my husband was exactly where he was meant to be. Embarrassed? A little, but much too tired to dwell on that. I was more worried he would continue to try to find ways to leave that place of despair. After that call, I knew sleep wouldn't come easily or quickly, if at all.

*****

Every day began as a mystery and ended the same way. No two days were the same. Often he refused to eat or drink anything, which led to an emergency hospital stay due to severe dehydration. His stay that time lasted five days. At home, he was always so cold even under five blankets and quilts stacked on top of him from chin to toe. And sometimes, in the middle of the night, usually around three o'clock in the morning, he would get out of bed, go downstairs in the dark, and sit in his favorite chair. He'd stay there for only a few minutes, then come back upstairs to bed. Still in the dark.

There seemed to be no reason for these pilgrimages. He couldn't tell me why he went. He simply had to do it. I was afraid he would tumble down the stairs in the darkened house because he had already been diagnosed as a "fall risk" throughout his three-year illness. These trips occurred, of course, while I was asleep, awakening only when he returned to bed. So I had to figure out how I'd know when he would leave the bedroom. I needed to wake up and try to stop him—which I could never do. He was adamant. He was determined. He was sick. So he went.

My "fix" was to close and lock our bedroom door before getting into bed. When he opened it at three o'clock, I would hear the click of the button lock, waking me up. Together we would navigate the stairs—he still insisted no lights be turned on. He'd go sit in his chair in the sunroom. I'd stretch out on the sofa in the family room facing him so I'd be ready to go back up the stairs to bed with him. This part of the almost nightly ritual was over. For tonight. Who knew what tomorrow night would bring?

*****

Cooking, usually my safe place, my haven, became a chore I didn't relish because my husband refused to eat. Nothing tasted good. I fed him a few bites anyway while he groused. He wasn't a good patient. I tried to understand and be patient because his mind still didn't grasp what was wrong. That understanding, though, didn't make me feel more charitable toward him during his most stubborn moments. I needed rest. I needed my husband back.

Thank God for family. It seemed that whenever I was beginning to feel completely overwhelmed, my family from Texas or my sons from Virginia and Georgia would visit and take charge of some of the things that needed to be done. For a little while, I was no longer alone with this man I didn't recognize and who didn't recognize himself.

*****

Gradually, he improved. It took quite a while, but trust started to return, so I could relax my vigilance and worry a little less. He seemed to be slowly returning to his old self, but I was afraid to believe it, to count on it. If he returned to that place of not knowing who or where he was, the disappointment would have been more than I could have borne. So it probably took a little longer than was absolutely necessary for me to completely believe in him again. I had

36

to be sure. I had to protect myself. I honestly don't believe I could endure again any of those long, heartbreaking months of worry and loneliness and fear.

Eventually, I believed.

CHAPTER 11

*Yea, mine own familiar friend, in whom I trusted, which
did eat of my bread, hath lifted up his heel against me.*

—Psalm 41:9

2016

We said we were best friends and would always be. Forever. Years
before that silly BFF acronym became so ubiquitous. We called each
other "sister." She didn't have a blood-related sister, and maybe I had
more than most, but none who exactly shared the same interests that
she and I did. And anyway, they all lived so far away.

We were both mothers of two children. In fact, that was how we
met. Our sons were in the same grade and became best friends—they
had a mutual story. My son had just transferred to that new school,
and so had hers. Friendship was the product of two new students
finding each other to create their own little team. After all, no one
wants to eat alone in a new cafeteria where everyone else seems to
have known each other since birth.

I trusted her completely. And I believe she would say that she
trusted me as well. As families, we began to do almost everything
together—we vacationed, spent Thanksgivings, and exchanged
Christmas gifts. We played cards and other board games, spent
almost every weekend doing something together at one of our homes.
It didn't matter whose home; it just mattered that we were together.
Laughing, eating, telling stories, and planning our next get-togeth-
ers. She was my emergency contact for my children's schools if my
husband and I couldn't be reached, and I was hers. I never once won-

dered if she would be there if she was needed. I knew she would. I knew her.

I thought.

*****

Years passed with life going on as it does. I had no idea anything would ever change. There was no reason. To me, true friends are like impenetrable vaults for each other. Literally, anything and everything can be put into that place with the secure assurance that nothing will be divulged. Ever. My deepest fears and worries, her most terrible experiences and memories—all of it is safe. The good and the not so good. Our vaults would contain all of our cares, dreams, worries, and fears. All held securely in the hands you trusted.

There's an old Black hymn that speaks of "laying your burdens down." That's what a friend's vault represents to me. The ability to unburden myself so that my mind can be a little less cluttered, my spirit a little stronger. It represents safety and unconditional understanding. And it is my duty, my privilege, and sacred oath to do the same for her.

But once that trust is broken, it can never be fully repaired. That's what happened to me. I thought my confidences were safe. I thought she cared enough about me to never share with anyone what I had shared with her. I certainly never believed—or even imagined—that she would fabricate stories that were not true and spread them to others in our circle of friends. And once confronted with my questions about that betrayal, I wasn't prepared for a denial that we both knew was false. I'd hoped for an apology, a request for forgiveness. She offered neither. Turns out, ending a friendship takes far less time and effort than starting one.

The hurt never really goes away. It is just tucked away. For a time, I mourned the loss of that friendship. It felt almost like a death. The sadness is there, but like death, you don't get to change the outcome. You live with it and learn from it.

*****

I don't know when, or even how, things changed, but I found a new friendship. I wasn't looking for it. I found it in a person I'd known and worked with for years. A strong bond between us had already been forged through our mutual collaboration in our work. We respected the contributions we each made to get the job done well. I admired her unparalleled creativity. She admired my no-nonsense approach toward management. We learned from each other even without realizing it.

What an unlikely pairing we are. Physically and culturally, we couldn't be more different. She is a fiery redhead with freckles. I'm not. She is the daughter of a doctor. My father had to put us on welfare for a time just so we could eat.

Eventually, when our conversations turned away from work and toward family, morality, and core values, we were a perfect match. And I believe that because we each already thought highly of the other, that usually awkward phase of getting to know each other was avoided. We simply enjoyed the same things and our beliefs aligned perfectly. We already trusted each other with work-related things and as individuals, so trust in our new friendship was easy.

*****

I met this extraordinary woman through our work. At the time, I had recently been recruited to become the vice president of sales and marketing for a large national homebuilder. She was an interior designer whose company decorated new models for national builders. We had never worked together, though. We hadn't even heard of each other; our paths had never crossed. Until one day. A couple of days after my arrival at the new homebuilding company, I was tasked by my president to find out why our company's homes weren't selling nearly as well as our competitor's next door. It was particularly concerning because our sales prices were lower than theirs.

I drove to that community alone. I wanted no other voices in my head—no other ideas or suggestions. I walked through our models first. There were three. Then I walked through the models of our competitor. The differences between the emotions and feelings those two walk-throughs evoked were polar opposites. Ours made no emotional impact at all. Although newly decorated, they felt dated and washed-out. It was difficult to remember anything specific about my company's homes. They were not special.

By contrast, the moment I entered the competition's models, I was transported—not to another time or place, but to a different emotional plane. The colors were vibrant but understated and tasteful. The furnishings and fabrications were elegant without being pretentious. The feeling they evoked was aspirational. They made you feel as though you should simply pack your clothes and move in. No changes necessary.

Who was this creative genius? I found her business card in a small holder near the front door. I called her immediately once I returned to my office. I asked for a meeting as soon as her schedule allowed.

The rest, as they say, is history. Our collaboration began that day, and working together, we improved my company's market share year over year, from fourth place when I arrived to first place. And that's where we stayed.

*****

To this day, I remain amazed by her vision and by her ability to translate that vision into something reminiscent of art. I am still in awe of her attention to every small detail and of her talent and humility.

Even though I've known her for years, it hasn't been as long as the friend I lost. But I feel as though I've known her my entire life. I believe she feels the same. I'm blessed to have her in my life, and I treasure her for giving back to me the one thing I thought never to regain…that purity of unquestioned love and acceptance between two women who truly respect and admire each other. Who know they are each better off for knowing the other.

CHAPTER 12

*For I was hungered, and ye gave me meat: I was thirsty, and
ye gave me drink: I was a stranger, and ye took me in.*
—Matthew 25:35

1963

I remember Christmas that year. I was fifteen years old. My father
had fallen fourteen feet at his commercial construction job several
months before, and he could not walk. He had broken his back.

We gamely put up our years old Christmas tree made of green-
painted aluminum. It looked slightly sad and a little worn out. Years
earlier, my father bought it on sale at Sears and Roebuck because he
knew we couldn't afford to buy a new, real tree every year. We decorated it with our discount store ornaments and tinsel that we saved
from year to year. I thought it was beautiful.

Because my father wasn't able to work, we weren't expecting Christmas gifts. Actually, we weren't expecting anything at all, including a big Christmas dinner. We would just observe the day with a prayer and whatever food my mother would put together—she always found something. And by then, we had been taught to be grateful for whatever God provided. And we were. No questions asked. No temper tantrums. We all understood. We knew we didn't have much, but we were still proud. We were all together, and that was all that mattered.

*****

I remember my older brothers and I had just gotten home from school—we were all in high school then. My younger siblings were playing outside. All of a sudden, they ran into the house to tell my mother and father that a "white lady" had just driven up and stopped at our house. No one who looked like her ever came into our neighborhood. Why would they? My parents had no idea who this visitor could be, but they were ready to welcome whoever it was into our very modest home.

A soft knock on the door. My mother answered, and there stood someone none of us recognized immediately. She introduced herself and seemed to know my mother's name. She called her Mrs. Brown. She offered her name—Mrs. Brinkley. I recognized that name as did my mother, father, and brothers. She lived in the richest neighborhood where my father and brothers mowed yards on weekends. She had been one of their customers for years and knew of his accident. She had come alone into the ghetto that was our home. She was unafraid.

She struggled with a huge basket, and my brothers quickly went to help her. That magical basket contained so much food—everything we would need for a proper holiday dinner. Everything from a turkey ready for roasting to potatoes and cream for mashing, to all the other fixings even down to tart and sweet cranberries for that sauce that completes every Christmas dinner.

I remember what she wore—a shirtwaist dress that was the color of blue birds. I've always loved clothes. I remember how she smelled—like summer flowers and clean linen dried under a sunny sky. I remember her smile that included all of us. We all smiled back. But most of all, I remember the respect and deference she showed my father. I remember a kind of sisterhood she seemed to share with my mother. Her eyes said all of that without a word being spoken. I will always remember her kindness, generosity, and courage. I didn't realize it then, but courage is what it took for her to visit us that day. I will never forget.

*****

I'd never seen my father cry. Until that moment. He couldn't stand up to greet her or to thank her properly as she left, so we stood up for him. She took our picture then, with our old Polaroid camera, standing in front of that aluminum tree with its cheap ornaments. As she gave the picture to my mother, they hugged as though they'd known each other for years—as women who are wives and mothers tend to do. Those women who are the backbone of every family, who understand the world intuitively and speak with a common language no one else can understand. She turned to leave. Her work here was done.

I watched as she drove away on that shale- and gravel-covered road. No pavement here. White dust rose like a mist behind her car, making the entire encounter seem ethereal. Almost spiritual.

*****

My memory of that day, the selfless kindness of a stranger, informs the way I think about and deal with the world as it is today. Now, when I start to despair about the state of our country and the world—with people spewing hate and distrust simply because we don't all look the same—I am comforted by my memory of that Christmas so long ago, when one person showed such kindness and grace.

I still remember her. I always will.

CHAPTER 13

And God blessed them, saying, "Be fruitful, and multiply, and fill the waters in the seas, and let fowl multiply in the earth."
—Genesis 1:22

December 1974

I'm pregnant. I found out just before Christmas but haven't told my husband yet. That's going to be one of his gifts under our small tree—a tiny gift box with a handwritten note inside.

I never thought about motherhood as a question. Maybe it's because I come from a very large family. I always believed I would have children, maybe three. Of course, then, after the actual birth of the first child, I was rethinking having even a second. But thankfully, after a time, memories of the pain and challenges of childbirth fade, and I was ready to do it all over again. The result is worth the pain. It's worth everything. And anyway, the second time is so much better, simply because the process is no longer a mystery. And those tiny faces are the most beautiful sights God ever created. It's the closest I'll probably ever come to experiencing a true miracle.

*****

Christmas day finally arrived. I couldn't stop smiling. I was not sure how long my secret would be safe with *me*! My husband and I exchanged gifts—several small things we needed and a few we didn't. I made sure to hide his "special" gift at the very back of the tree, ensuring it would be the last one he opens.

I'd wrapped it with special care, which means I'd used almost an entire roll of adhesive tape on that small box. It took my bewildered husband forever to open it. By now, I was grinning so broadly my cheeks began to hurt. I couldn't seem to stop. I almost blurted out what it was he was trying so determinedly to open. Finally, success. My husband's reaction was exactly right. It was just what I'd hoped it would be…a warm, full embrace that left his tears on my cheeks and mine on his. This child would be our first together.

*****

This moment was profoundly important and meaningful to me because, before I conceived, I consulted with a gynecologist to be sure I was healthy and that conception and childbirth would be a normal process. This doctor was from "The Old School" which meant he was old himself. He was a white-haired white man with stooped shoulders and zero bedside manner. He always appeared to be in a hurry—too busy to ask or answer questions. He seemed to be in constant "flight" mode whenever we were together. He was clearly uncomfortable and didn't try to hide it. Maybe he couldn't.

After his examination, which felt somewhat perfunctory to me, he met with me in his office. There, he informed me I had something called fibroid tumors. I had no idea what that was or what it meant. And his deep, measured tone made his diagnosis sound even more ominous. I asked him what the fix would be and how long it would take before I would be able to conceive.

As though he was delivering a pronouncement from God, he said, "There's absolutely nothing to be done. No cure. You will need a total hysterectomy." *What!* How did I go from being a healthy twenty-six-year-old who'd never had a bad examination or diagnosis, to a twenty-six-year-old who needed a total hysterectomy? His words clanged in my head like discordant notes from a band whose members had never met before. Nothing made sense. He made no sense.

He had no answers to my questions and no patience for explanations he felt were unnecessary. And as far as he was concerned, probably above my intellectual capacity to understand anyway. After all, he was the "learned" doctor. Apparently, I had no right to question his judgment or his diagnosis. Period. I couldn't speak. I couldn't move. I could only stare at him. I stared so long that he was finally forced to look directly at me.

In that moment, I immediately understood. He wasn't interested in bringing a child into the world who looked like me. That realization mobilized me. I stood, collected my belongings, and walked away. No other words were spoken. There was nothing left to say.

Clearly, I needed a second opinion. Hopefully, this time from an unbiased doctor. I consulted a different doctor referred to me by a friend and coworker I trusted—another white man but younger and kind. Almost everything the previous doctor had said was turned on its head. For starters, the examination was more thorough. He asked questions and listened to mine with interest. His diagnosis confirmed that I did indeed have fibroid tumors, but they were small and could be easily removed. He discussed a treatment plan, which would allow me to be able to have the family I'd always wanted.

I learned an important lesson that day. Life choices—those most important hopes and dreams—can never be taken for granted. And you should never give up on them without a fight and the most information you can find.

My husband got me through this harrowing time. He was always there, taking me to my doctor's appointments and caring for me.

The treatment plan was set. Several months after the surgery that removed those awful fibroid tumors, my doctor declared that not only was I able to conceive, but I was actually already pregnant and should have a worry-free pregnancy and delivery. I felt on top of the world—except for occasional morning sickness. Until.

One day at work, I noticed spots of blood where there shouldn't have been any. I made an emergency appointment with my doctor who explained that I was in danger of miscarrying. There was no apparent reason. In an abundance of caution, his prescription was complete bed rest for a solid week. Standing upright was forbidden. To prevent a miscarriage, I had to be carried everywhere. In a matter of minutes, my world shrank to our bedroom and bathroom. My husband carrying me and caring for me like a frail, sick child. He was always there.

We finally got through that week. At my next appointment, my doctor was very pleased with my progress. The worst was over. The three of us had made it through intact.

*****

New discoveries. Once I became a parent, I found myself seemingly going to every kind of sports game known to humankind. Little, short people running as hard as they know how, trying to kick a ball into a net that's being "guarded" by another short person who seems to be more interested in the clouds; or trying to hit a small plastic ball, perched on a stick, with a plastic bat and then forgetting to run to first base. Never mind, he completely missed the ball anyway. They keep trying, though. And they finally succeed… sometimes.

For me, motherhood is an incredible phenomenon that I suspect only other mothers can understand. I found myself rooting for all of those precious children—no matter which team they were playing on. They were all trying their hardest, with pinched, focused faces even though they knew their reward at the end of all of that energetic trying would only be orange slices and water…and heaps of praise from all the moms and dads. It didn't matter. They were grass-stained, sweaty warriors, and I'm sure those orange slices tasted like victory. No matter who won.

To this day, I continue to root for my sons no matter what they do even though they are men now. To me, they will forever be those short people trying their hardest.

*****

Becoming a mother made me more patient, gave me more empathy. Of course, there's no manual that comes with that cute, helpless newborn who's totally dependent on me to get things right.

There's no guide to tell me what to do, what to expect, or how to cope. What I did have, though, was the wonderful example set by my mother for me to follow.

And that was enough.

CHAPTER 14

The Lord maketh poor, and maketh rich: He bringeth low, and lifteth up. He raiseth up the poor out of the dust, and lifteth up the beggar from the dunghill, to set them among princes, and to make them inherit the throne of glory: for the pillars of the earth are the Lord's, and he hath set the world upon them.
—1 Samuel 2:7–8

1960s

Acres Home. That's the name of the area in the northern part of Houston, Texas, where I grew up. The name sounds so grand, evoking visions of large homes on even larger plots of land—acres, in fact. In reality, the name says exactly what it was and is: a lot of very small houses built snuggly together, one after another on a large swath of land, also known as acreage. Someone had a sense of humor.

Growing up there, I knew I never wanted to stay there. There had to be more to life than the simple and complex desperation of surviving day-to-day, hoping for miracles that never came. Surely, there was a way for me to leave this place, never to return. It wasn't that it was a bad place to grow up. Actually, it was fun—filled with families just like mine who were trying to live peacefully and raise families the best they could. I didn't know we were poor because everyone was poor, so there were no contrasts to be made. There was a proud community spirit where neighbors helped neighbors. Where children played outside until darkness drove us inside to our almost identical homes.

*****

From Mondays to Fridays, our family ate the same thing—pinto beans and corn bread. My mother would find creative and inexpensive ways to make the beans taste just a little different every day—adding a piece of salt pork one day, a ham hock another. On Saturdays, my father brought home burgers from his second job. A treat worth waiting for!

But on Sundays, we always had chicken that was fried, rice with gravy, and green peas from a can, which all of us kids secretly hated. Every now and then, we even had dessert—berry dumplings made from the bounty of little plastic buckets filled with black or red berries we'd picked from the empty lot up the street.

*****

I remember one Sunday, the mother of our next-door neighbor sent one of her sons to our house. He had a note for my mother. After reading it, my mother, without hesitation or thought, put together a small box of food, gave it to the little boy, and sent him on his way back home.

Somehow, that particular Sunday, my mother shared exactly half of our supper. My siblings and I didn't know that, because we all ate enough food to get full. I can still hear my mother's admonishment as we fixed our plates, "Just get one piece of a chicken for now and see if that's enough. You can come back if you're still hungry." None of us went back for seconds. Miraculously, we were all full enough.

My father's plate was always made first. My mother always ate last. I suppose she ate whatever was left on our plates to augment the backbone of the chicken she always kept for herself, saying it was her favorite part. I didn't know it then, but I do now—that wasn't her favorite part—it was just the part that was left. The part no one else wanted, that had the least amount of yield compared to the effort it took to find it.

They say children learn more by watching what you do than by listening to what you say. I believe that saying because, to this day,

I make my plate last. After I'm sure everyone has gotten as much as they want.

That Sunday night, two families were fed. We'll worry about tomorrow, tomorrow.

*****

I have always been an eager learner—never satisfied with partial answers or half-truths. I always wanted to know "more." In high school, my favorite class was home economics. Not because of the actual subject matter, which didn't interest me at all. I already knew how to sew and cook. It was the teacher of that class who intrigued me. I wanted to learn from her things that weren't in the curriculum. Things like how to dress properly. I loved mixing and matching outfits to make a new look—a desire born out of necessity when all you have are bits and pieces left over from your older sister. I wanted to learn which fork to use and where to place the knife after cutting meat. Surely, it doesn't go back onto the clean tablecloth! She wore makeup! No one in my family did, so what exactly did the big world of makeup entail? This teacher would unlock all of those mysteries for me. She became my mentor when I didn't even know that was a word.

I wish I had known then how to tell her what she meant to me. I wish I had thanked her for allowing me to feel comfortable in unfamiliar settings as I ventured out into the world.

CHAPTER 15

*Behold, how good and how pleasant it is for
brethren to dwell together in unity!*

—Psalm 133:1

Summers

It's summertime. No more school, no more homework, and best of all, no more socks and shoes. And no more getting up early and despairing that I haven't studied long or hard enough for the history test in second period. But especially, no anxiety over seeing "him"—the boy of my dreams—in the hallway, hoping and then not hoping today he will notice me.

There's always enough sunlight to play outside barefoot and carefree until exhaustion finally wins. It always wins, but testing those limits every day is sheer delight. We'll finish the game tomorrow…because there's always tomorrow, or so it seemed at the time.

"Be careful! No playing in the street," our mother called out to us. That street, of course, is the only place we want to play, my brothers, sisters, and me. "We'll be at the park soon enough," she said.

Summertime is always the best…Sunday's fried chicken dinners with a watermelon, bought and sliced right off the back of the "watermelon man's" truck. Sweet, sticky juice runs down brown, grinning faces. No one notices. No one cares.

Finally, we're here. The neighborhood county park. There are no "amenities" like sliding boards or swing sets. We don't miss them because we've never had them. It doesn't matter, though, because little children always find ways to make their own fun. Freshly mown grass, meat marinated overnight slowly roasting on a homemade grill, laughing children chasing each other, adults playing cards and not worrying about their rambunctious offspring. I think heaven must sound and smell like this—our family reunions. There is one every summer.

There's nothing quite like a family reunion in the South. Parents and grandparents, aunts, uncles, and cousins, some of whom you don't really know or recognize, congregate together as one huge free-flowing familial amoeba. Every year we meet at the same pre-determined place and time in that county park. It's kind of become our spot. Every family seems to have their favorite place, and this one is ours.

It's situated under a large pecan tree that offers welcome shade from the unrelenting sun. Rarely anyone, especially the children, stays put under that tree. Of course, there're picnic tables and benches, but no one seems inclined to sit. Everyone will settle there at that long table once lunch is ready. There's a lot to do to get food on the table.

The mission is the same every year—enjoy great company, tasty food, and exhausting activities. Everyone is involved—young and old. My mother and all of my aunts bring something to contribute to the menu. Some dishes are more welcomed than others, but no one goes home hungry.

Someone's little one gets bumped and falls down. It doesn't matter who the child belongs to. Mothers from every direction converge en masse to be sure the injury is not fatal and that no blood is leaking from anywhere. Once determined the only trauma is hurt pride and nothing more, the child's eyes are dried and immediately returned to the game, whatever it was. Every child here is happy, knowing they're being watched over even though every mother is busy with other things. Maybe that's where the word multitasking got its popularity. Mothers have done it for centuries and forever will.

*****

All the young men, including my brothers, get to the park early to set up their grills and start the long, slow process of cooking all the main dishes: several large slabs of pork ribs, beef briskets, chickens, and sausages. Too many to count. My older brother makes his "famous" barbecue sauces. Yes, there's more than one kind. He takes so much pride in being able to make sauces for any palate—from mild to spicy—and even one made with coffee. I've tasted each one, just in case he needs an "expert" opinion, and I have declared all three to be excellent! I was in charge of the Kool-Aid punch, which I "doctored up" with sherbet and ginger ale. It tasted like summer to me. Fun and refreshing. Later, when I was old enough to contribute cooked dishes, one of my younger sisters took over Kool-Aid duty.

*****

There are so many large coolers: one filled with potato salad, pasta salad, and other cold dishes; another for water and soft drinks; and one for hot dishes like macaroni and cheese, baked beans, and so many others. And then the desserts: peach cobbler, tea cakes (which are really just large vanilla cookies), pies, and banana pudding. And my sister's showstopper: a sock-it-to-me cake. No one knows how that cake got its name or even what it means, but that cake is darned good. And there's never any left.

Conversations flow around each and every one of us—no one really knowing or caring who is talking to whom. There is music just loud enough for us to enjoy without disturbing our nearest neighbor. Along with running, screaming children, there are dancing and singing contests, posing for pictures, games being played, and laughter… lots of laughter.

Everything is noisy, comforting, and comfortable. It's officially summertime.

CHAPTER 16

For David is not ascended into the heaven: but he saith himself, The Lord said unto my Lord, Sit thou on my right hand, Until I make thy foes thy footstool.

—Acts 2:34–35

1966–2006

At the age of eighteen, my new world began with college. Seventeen thousand five hundred students. The five hundred part represented the total number of Black students. What a different world—from my all-Black elementary, junior high, and high schools, and neighborhood to a virtually all-White university. All new experiences every day. I loved it.

****

While I was completing my senior year in college, I was recruited by Mobil Oil to work in their corporate headquarters in Dallas, Texas. And since then, I've never had to look for a job until my brother died, and my small family moved from Connecticut back to Texas. Otherwise, jobs tended to find me. People called headhunters would contact me for new opportunities. Sometimes I said yes. Other times I didn't. Ironically, the one job I had to look for was the one that brought me into the homebuilding industry—the industry in which I would serve throughout the remainder of my career.

****

The early years in that industry brought stints in human resources, sales, and construction management. Years passed; promotions came. New opportunities were offered by larger national and international homebuilding companies. The more senior the position, the greater the responsibilities and obligations—to team members, customers, and shareholders. My commitment to each step on my personal ladder was undeniable. I would always strive to do the very best job I could. Always. Because…"if you're not going to do something well, then don't do it at all." My father's words will always ring in my ears. They ring true to who I was and to who I have become.

The lessons from my father of always doing your best no matter what, learned so long ago, paved the way for me to eventually become an executive vice president for a major international homebuilder—the builder of the Olympic arena in Greece, where the corporate headquarters were located. I became a member of the executive committee, which provided the opportunity for me to make presentations to the board of directors.

It allowed me to set the goals and objectives for my areas of responsibility, the Mid-Atlantic Region, which consisted of several divisions in many cities and states. I was given the authority to manage hundreds of team members, oversee thousands of new homes' construction and delivery to customers, and contribute many millions of dollars in revenue and bottom-line profitability. It allowed me to train and manage some of the best and brightest in the industry.

I led every division under my command from last place in customer satisfaction in the entire company when I arrived, to being the best in the company when I left. That was, in fact, my greatest personal achievement—going from worst place to first place in this tremendously important initiative—because it took all of us: contractors, employees, and management working together toward a common goal, delivering a product that we could all be proud of.

And most of all, to keep the promise we had made to our customers who had placed their trust in us.

*****

"I don't believe He brought me this far to leave me. I've come too far from where I started from." This old hymn was one of my favorites growing up in our small Baptist church. The choir led the entire congregation in song as we all stood with voices raised in praise. With eyes closed and faces lifted toward heaven, we sang. And we believed those words that were so sacred to us. Those words became my strength, my talisman. I hung onto them when I was called a n—gger bitch by a fellow salesperson when I beat her out of her years-long grip on the title of Top Producer. I hung onto them when, as a construction manager, I was told by a home inspector that he wouldn't inspect my homes because I was "taking the food off the table of a white man." Of course, my family needed to eat too, but clearly that wasn't his concern.

And I hung onto those words when I was passed over for a promotion to division president that rightfully—based solely on performance—should have been mine. But I was told to "wait my turn" while that promotion went to a much less qualified white man. And those words helped me find the right words to rebuff a sexual advance from my white boss and still keep my job.

Yes, I needed that song. Throughout my life, it was a constant reminder that my blessings came from God through my hard work. And I had no intention of allowing others to define me, to pigeonhole me. To stop me. The more they tried to push me aside, to diminish my accomplishments, or ignore me completely, the harder I fought for my place, my contributions. My honor.

I was able to achieve heights I didn't even know existed. I didn't know how to dream that big. What I did know is this: through it all, I remained at heart a little Black girl from Acres Home striving to become someone more. Someone exceptional.

CHAPTER 17

Yea, though I walk through the valley of the shadow of death, I will fear no evil: for thou art with me; thy rod and thy staff they comfort me.
—Psalm 23:4

1953–Present Day

"The Lord is my shepherd; I shall not want. Remember to say those words whenever you leave home." That was my mother's admonishment whenever we ventured out into the world. Whether we were driving back to college after visiting home for a long weekend or flying away to some exotic vacation years later. My mother made sure that lesson was engrained in all of us. "Say the twenty-third Psalms," she'd say. I think it was meant to be our talisman against everything evil in this world—from traffic accidents to airplane crashes to policemen with guns. We would be safe as long as we said those precious words.

My mother taught all of her children, and all of her children have taught ours that same lesson.

*****

I wake up feeling a little apprehensive every morning. I always have, even when I was little. I don't know where this feeling comes from or why it's so constant. Is it intuition or something more spiritual, like visions?

I remember when I was five years old, I would wake up in the middle of the night. Unable to go back to sleep, I would go to my parents' room and lie at the foot of their bed. Having eleven children meant there was always a baby in bed with them, so the foot of the bed was the only available space for a scared little girl. I didn't mind at all. My mother knew why I was there—my mother knew everything—and she would tell me to say my prayers again. I would, and almost immediately, precious sleep would be my reward. I felt safe.

*****

I'm a worrier by nature. Apparently, I'm not very good at just letting things happen, assuming they will work out just fine or, failing that, they'll work themselves out without intervention from me. That theory may or may not be true, but that truth doesn't set me free. It keeps me on edge. Control is what I crave—it keeps me sane in an insane world.

I've heard the saying, "Worry is imagination misused." For me, though, imagining the worst that could happen keeps me prepared to cope, to handle anything that comes my way. But it also robs me of unfettered joy and ignorant bliss. And unfortunately, my imagination is very fertile ground, and it never rests.

Every morning when I wake up, I take stock of everything and everyone in my life, making sure there's no feeling of impending doom associated with a name or an event. I've been known to call my husband or one of my sons to tell them to be extra watchful for things unseen and unknown. They always indulged me and would sometimes tell me later that because of their extra vigilance, some danger was avoided. And because my husband and sons would never lie to preserve my feelings, I knew their recounted stories were true. Of course, all that did was solidify my need for constant vigilance. But candidly, I didn't need an excuse. That's just how I'm made.

*****

I believe that the need to ensure every aspect of life that can be controlled is as harnessed as it can be, made me a better manager. It allowed me to view all sides of an issue objectively, looking for, and usually finding, a weakness or flaw that could derail the project. Avoiding those pitfalls ensured the best results possible and were quantifiable and understandable to those responsible for executing the project. We planned for the worst-case scenario while hoping for the best possible outcome. But my strong belief is this: Hope is not a plan. My sentiment is, "If you have a plan, and work the plan, the plan will work for you."

This approach dominated my life throughout my career, and it still does. Having a plan allows for a clearer mind, a better quality of sleep, even for me. It changes nothing that "could" happen, but I rest secure in the knowledge that I have done everything in my power to ensure the outcome we planned for is realized. There's nothing else to be done. There's comfort in that knowledge. And sleep comes a little easier.

I still wake up in the middle of the night. I still wonder what I might lose today. Or who do I have to be brave for? Maybe myself? And I still say my prayers to get back to sleep.

*****

Some call it fate or intuition. I call it faith as the Bible describes it…*"Now faith is the substance of things hoped for, the evidence of things not seen."* As my mother taught me…"Through faith, all things are possible." I am thankful for those lessons learned through the examples set by my mother every day. And I am proud to be like her—a woman of faith.

Time for bed. Tomorrow will come soon enough, potentially bringing with it more things to worry about. I'll worry about those things tomorrow.

CHAPTER 18

*The Lord is near to the brokenhearted and
saves those who are crushed in spirit.*

—Psalm 34:18

1966

College. I thought I was ready for this particular new adventure. Sitting at home, safely aware of everyday routines and familiar faces was my refuge. It's time to leave this place of comfortable sameness. Now that it's finally time to go, I'm feeling pretty nervous. I'm going four hours away from home to a place where I don't know anyone or what to expect. I've dreamt about this moment so many times. I thought I would be completely ready when the time came for me to leave home and fly on my own. I was wrong.

Throughout my young life, I've been taught many lessons about how to comport myself in any given situation. But I've never been in a situation like this before. I've never lived with anyone but my family. I've never had to manage my own life completely, from handling money from the loan I got to afford to go to this school, to knowing which classes to take.

My high school didn't have guidance counselors to provide helpful advice and, well, actual guidance. I guess there wasn't enough money in the school's budget, or maybe someone thought that kind of expenditure would be wasted on a school in our neighborhood.

Because I'd always helped out with my siblings and ailing father while going to high school and juggling my two church jobs, I'm not afraid of hard work. I knew I would have to get at least one job to help pay my school expenses. The loan only covered tuition, so books, room and board, and incidentals were up to me to figure out. I ended up having to get three jobs—serving dinner in my dorm's cafeteria every night, listening to "mean girls" being themselves; typing papers and tests for professors in the School of Business on Mondays, Wednesdays, and Fridays; and on Thursdays and Saturdays, selling clothes in an upscale lady's boutique located at the edge of campus.

*****

I remember my mother and me being driven to the campus by our across-the-street neighbors. The trip took just over four hours but seemed like only a few minutes. I wasn't prepared to say goodbye to my mother. I wouldn't see her again until Thanksgiving, which, in August, seemed to be light years away. All of my belongings were packed and stowed in the trunk of the car. They didn't take up much space, but it was all I had.

*****

I'd already imagined what would happen once we got to my assigned dormitory room: my mother and I would unload the car's trunk, take everything upstairs to my room, and unpack. We would make the bed together, giggling like a couple of schoolgirls on a new adventure. I loved thinking about that part of the trip the most.

Too soon, I'm unpacked, and it's time for my mother and neighbors to head back home. I thanked our neighbors for their help and promised to keep in touch. I hugged my mother and in that moment, seemed unable to let go. I clung to her, crying into her shoulder. She was misty-eyed too, but her composure didn't completely desert her. It never did. She kissed my tear-streaked cheek and told me to remember to pray. Then she left. I could only watch as they drove away.

I didn't realize it then, but I literally started running down the street after their car, silent tears streaming down my face. I wasn't aware I was making a spectacle of myself. I wouldn't have cared anyway. I felt deserted in a foreign place. I just wanted my mother to stay with me. But she couldn't. I understood that in my head, but my heart seemed to have a mind of its own. I finally realized what I was doing and stopped in the middle of the street. I watched as their car slowly receded out of view. I couldn't see my mother any longer, but I imagined her looking out of the rear windshield already missing me too. I turned around, slowly walked back to my new home, and started on my newest journey. Alone.

Once I got back to my dorm room, I felt a little more composed. My tears had dried, and I was determined to stay strong like I had always been taught to do. I met my roommates. There were two. Although I didn't know her well, one was a girl I had grown up with in church. We didn't go to the same high school, but we did have a lot of the same experiences—coming from neighborhoods that were like bookends to each other. Seeing her made me feel a little less alone. The other girl was from Dallas and seemed more worldly to me somehow. She was ridiculously smart and funny. I liked her immediately. We were all Black, and I remember wondering if that was a purposeful arrangement. I'm pretty sure I knew the answer. The three of us lived, ate, and studied together. And we learned how to manage in this new world. We were the support system for each other.

Some weekends, when my roommates and I didn't have a lot of homework to complete, the three of us would go to my Dallas roommate's parents' home. Those times were so special to me. They reminded me of being at home with my mother. We cooked dinner with her mother, we met her other siblings, and everything felt like home.

She became my very best friend. We met when we were only eighteen-year-old girls with similar dreams. Ultimately, our friendship lasted more than fifty years before she died of cancer. I visited her just a few months before that horrific news came and was honored when she asked me to cook a meal for her. She knew exactly what she wanted: the same meal I'd made for her homecoming after the birth of her first child: potato salad, buttermilk fried chicken, and peach cobbler. I was happy to cook anything and everything for her. We loved each other like sisters.

I still miss her. I always will.

CHAPTER 19

1966

While in college, I worked three jobs simultaneously because my ability to stay there depended on those earnings, as well as getting a student loan every school year. When I could, I sent a little money home to help my mother and siblings. When I applied for a loan for summer school after my freshman year, I had to wait to find out if the loan would be honored. It took longer than I had planned. I couldn't enroll in summer school until I received those funds, which meant enrolling at the last minute. That problem also meant I could not choose my roommate. I had to take whatever space was left. I was assigned to a room with another girl I didn't know and who didn't seem to want to know me. Ironically, her first name was the same as mine. Easy to remember.

*****

One evening around eight o'clock, Cora, the roommate, asked if I would accompany her to an apartment just off campus to retrieve a book. She needed it for a class the next day. Or so she said. It was summertime in Texas, and it didn't get dark until late. I decided to do her a favor and go with her. I remember getting there, and my roommate went into a back room while I sat on the sofa in the living room and waited patiently. I didn't really think anything was out of the ordinary when she disappeared into that other room. I just sat there waiting for her to come back with her book.

How naive I was! Until that moment, I didn't know how sheltered my life had been and how trusting I was of people's intentions. I had been taught to trust. And I did—until I no longer could. That time was now.

Almost immediately after my roommate went into that back room, a man about my age came out of a second back room wearing only a small towel covering his midsection. Before I knew what was happening, he yanked me off the sofa and pushed me into the bedroom he'd just left. His stature was slight, not tall but wiry. I remember being completely shocked by his strength! He never said a word, but his intentions were crystal clear in that moment…the moment I began the fight of my life.

He threw me across the small room onto a bed. I fought for what felt like hours. I begged him to stop. And still, he didn't speak. That was every bit as unnerving as the assault itself. I fought until my strength began to wane. I remember praying out loud, "God, please help me, please help me!" My attacker finally spoke. His voice low and threatening, he said, "Even God can't help you now." Oh, how I wish he'd stayed silent! My spirit was broken with those six chilling words.

That was the moment I was ready to relent, to give up all hope. I was too tired. I was bleeding from scratches inflicted during the fight. The top of my dress had been torn, and I just wanted everything to be over.

Just when I felt all was lost, someone started banging on the bedroom door. Yelling that it was almost curfew, and I needed to be gotten out of there. Otherwise, both my attacker and I would be expelled. He got off me then—just in the nick of time. And I fled. My sandals, which had disappeared long ago, were left behind. I just ran, holding my torn dress together the best I could. I didn't spend any time looking for my new roomie as I ran out of there. It appeared she was nowhere to be found anyway. Later, I learned she had apparently left over an hour before, after spending time with some guy in the other bedroom. How could she have left me there? I knew she was able to hear me fighting, crying, and praying for help in that small apartment. But still, she left.

*****

Finally, I was back home—at my dorm where everything used to be familiar and safe. Right now, I didn't feel safe anywhere. I was starting to feel the physical effects of my fight for the survival of my innocence. I was exhausted and sore. My throat felt scratchy, and I couldn't seem to stop trembling. Worst of all, I felt unclean from the inside out.

And there she was. I found my roommate sitting on her bed reading a book. Maybe it was the book she supposedly needed to get. I doubt it. I knew in that moment I had been set up by her. She didn't, or couldn't, look at me. We both knew what had just happened.

Suddenly, someone down the hall yelled my name. A phone call had come in on the one communal phone located in the same place on each floor of the dorm. And it was for me. Who could be calling me? It was after curfew, after all. Still shaking uncontrollably, my voice sounded weak to my own ears when I said a small, "Hello?" Unbelievably, it was the perpetrator of my sexual assault! The second I answered, he began taunting me, saying I shouldn't be upset since *he's* the one who didn't get what he wanted. I was crying, shaking, confused. I was scared. Of course, that was his point. I hung up without saying another word. I don't think I could have spoken even if I'd tried.

*****

After a very long, hot shower, I called my mother. I needed to hear her voice. I needed her wisdom. I wanted to leave this place right now and go home where safety awaited me. My mother's voice was immediately comforting. Just hearing it made me calmer. She understood how extremely upset I had to be because I'd never quit anything before or shirked my responsibilities. She knew I needed to feel truly safe. I needed time—and a place to mentally heal from this trauma. That place was home. That place was her.

After my call with my mother, one thing became even more certain. I absolutely could not, would not, stay in this room with my roommate sleeping only a few feet away. I packed up everything I owned. That night, single suitcase in hand, I slept on the floor in the room of one of my true friends while her current roommate slept comfortably in her bed. I didn't need a bed. I just needed a temporary haven.

Just as my mother had promised, my brother borrowed a car from a friend of his who would one day become his brother-in-law. He drove those four hours to pick me up the very next morning. Time to start my journey toward healing.

*****

I returned to school in the fall. Stronger and no longer naive.

CHAPTER 20

I can do all things through Christ who strengthens me.
—Philippians 4:13

1976–2006

"Mommy!"

A bloodcurdling yell from my eight-year-old son. As I race upstairs, I imagine an entire scenario that has him lying helpless in a pool of blood. It seems to take forever, but I finally push through the door. I'm frantic. But there he stands, perfectly fine except he's shirtless.

"What's the emergency?" I ask once I'm able to speak.

"I can't find my soccer shirt, so I'll be late for my game!" he says calmly...now.

My heart is still beating wildly from my own worry and sprinting up the stairs. Deep breaths. Clearly, I need to do a better job of teaching him what a true emergency is.

"Your shirt is in the dryer downstairs, so don't worry. You'll be on time for your game."

"Honey, have you seen my keys? I don't remember where I put them last night," my husband asks. As I enter the kitchen again, I see them immediately.

"They're right here in the basket on the kitchen desk," I respond. Then under my breath, I say "Where they always are."

I wonder why it's easier to ask me when he's literally standing right in front of them. Habit, I guess, formed years ago before we had a kitchen desk and special basket for keys or anything else.

"Mom, will you take me to my friend's house, please?" Apparently, it's my older son's turn.

"Why?" I ask.

"We have a school project to finish before Monday." Of course, the project was assigned more than a week ago, but they've decided to wait until the last minute. No surprise there.

"Yes, I'll drive you over right after I finish cleaning up the breakfast dishes."

A ringing cell phone. It's mine. My boss is calling to tell me he doesn't like how he was quoted in an article in the *Washington Post's* Real Estate Section.

He says, through what I imagine are clenched teeth, "You need to call them and fix this."

He's fuming as if it's not already too late to fix anything. It's time to break the bad news to him.

Calmly, I respond, "If you're reading the article, it's already too late. Remember when I asked you not to take the interview without me, but you insisted? Since the article is written and published, there's absolutely nothing I can do." And now you've got to live with it. That last part was said after we'd hung up.

A typical Saturday morning in the life of a working wife and mother.

*****

"How do you do it? How do you juggle a career and family and not lose yourself?" I've been asked those questions so many times over the course of my career. My first thought is always, "The same way I do everything." Being a wife and mother is a daunting job, whether her work is inside or outside the home. Or both. Everyone depends on you to be dependable. Always.

Being a working wife and mother isn't easy. And since there's no "How To" manual for either of these important jobs, I approach both tasks similarly: through planning, communication, and execution. These elements are key both at home and at work. Equally important is ensuring that everyone involved knows what the mission is and what their particular role is, or will be, in completing that mission. You have to care enough to look at everything—both at work and home through the same lens; everything in both arenas demand the same level of importance.

*****

My job wasn't a typical eight-to-five, five-days-a-week kind of job. It was a however-long-it-takes-to-get-the-job-done kind of job, which meant being available and in charge twenty-four hours a day, seven days a week, three hundred and sixty-five days a year. I compare it to what I believe it must be like to be in the military or law enforcement. No matter how calm everything seemed, I always had to be in a state of readiness. Everything must be kept running smoothly—on time and on budget. That was my work ethic. My philosophy.

*****

During my career, one of my titles was executive vice president, and I reported directly to the president. I was his second-in-command. Said differently, I was his only responsibility and everyone else reported to me through their vice presidents. He had one person to worry about. Me. I had hundreds.

Once, as my boss was leaving for the night at six o'clock, I remember him stopping in the doorway of my office and telling me that I needed to get more balance in my life. Of course, he knew I would still be at my desk for at least another hour or so. I always was. I needed to tie up any loose ends from that day's business and be ready for the next day's issues—whatever they might be.

My response to him was simple, "You're able to have balance in your life *specifically because* I have none in mine."

He tilted his head to one side as if he was thinking, then nodded. And left. He knew there was nothing left to say.

"See you tomorrow."

*****

One important rule I lived by concerned my sons and husband. If either one of them called me, I would immediately excuse myself from whatever meeting I was in or project I was working on. I would always take their calls. My family and I had another standing rule. The boys had to call me when they got home from school or sports practices. I needed to know they were home safe and sound.

Otherwise, they could only call me if there was an emergency. They all knew the definition of an emergency by now—being hungry after school and wanting to know what they could eat most certainly was not one. Anyway, there were already "mom-approved" snacks in the house, and they knew it. The main objective of those rules was to be sure they knew I would be there for them when and if I was truly needed.

My husband and I were, and are, true partners in every sense of the word. His job was more conventional, in that he could usually leave work around the same time every day. When my older son went to university at the age of sixteen, his little brother was only twelve. I knew he was uneasy about being home alone in that big house, not knowing when someone would come home. So, together, we made a promise to our young son that one of us would always leave work by six—I would have to bring work home to finish up later—so he would only have to be alone and brave for a couple of hours. That knowledge gave my son the feeling of security that was exactly what he needed. He knew we would keep our word, and we did, all the way through his schooling until he graduated from high school.

*****

It didn't matter which parent got home first. The first one would start dinner. Leaving home in the morning, I would wear my slippers downstairs, leaving them in the laundry room where I changed into my heels. Once back home, I would make the opposite move, changing from my work shoes back into my slippers. Stepping into the kitchen while rolling up my sleeves and putting on my apron to protect my work clothes, I would either start or take over the dinner duties. By the time I finished washing my hands, my son would be downstairs to say hello, give me a welcome home smile, hug, and kiss.

While boiling potatoes or searing meat and deciding which green vegetable he would be forced to endure, homework needed to be checked. My husband and I had our strengths and weaknesses when it came to which subjects I would review and which ones belonged to him. He was the resident expert in all things math, history, geography, and French. I was responsible for English and grammar, biology, chemistry, Spanish, and spelling.

*****

When I grew up, my mother ensured that we always ate dinner together every night. That was our time to catch up with each other. I carried that same practice into my home. Every weeknight we all ate dinner together at the breakfast room table. We held hands, making an unbroken circle, and said grace. To this day, my sons still say grace before they eat.

We discussed our day, which included school for them and work for my husband and me. It was important for us to understand their lives and for them to understand ours. No TV was allowed. Thankfully, there weren't nearly as many electronic devices to distract them back then.

School lunches for the next day were prepared, sometimes from leftovers, and stored in the fridge in brown paper bags, their names indicating which bag belonged to which boy.

*****

I also knew how important it was for me to know which activities and events were important to my sons. The good news was that their school district was great when it came to sending out calendars with scheduled activities for the entire school year. What a valuable tool for parents—working or not. It allowed me to plan ways in which I could be a part of the most impactful moments in my sons' school lives. I was there when my older son competed in his wrestling championship match. I drove my youngest son to his middle school dance—I might have broken a couple of speed limits to make it home in time for him to jump into the car for the short ride to his school.

Golf tournaments, championship soccer, football, and baseball games, I was there. And of course, prom nights—taking pictures along with all the other proud parents. I was there. I hoped that when my sons looked back on those special moments, my presence would be part of their future memories.

*****

Being present and available as much as I could was very important to me. I needed to find ways to make small, normal things seem special. One creation was something I called Mommy/Baby Day Out. On weekends, for an entire day, each son would get to choose an activity that only the two of us would share. With my oldest, that always entailed a trip to the mall. My youngest and I would usually end up at the Putt-Putt golf course near our home. The boys never knew when a Mommy/Baby Day Out would occur, which made for unanticipated happiness when one was announced.

Another activity I created was called Midnight Run. At that time, one son had a bedtime of eight-thirty and the other nine o'clock. I would wait until around ten thirty or so, go into their rooms, quietly wake them up and tell them that it was Midnight Run time! The first time, I was greeted with confused, sleep-filled eyes. When they saw my grinning face, they suddenly understood—something fun was about to happen. Every time after, huge smiles greeted me. Sleep was totally forgotten for a time.

Of course, it was nowhere near midnight. They never asked what time it was. They just knew what that wake-up call meant—the three of us going into the family room after retrieving our very own pints of ice cream and spoons from the kitchen. Vanilla and cookies and cream for the boys, chocolate for me. Those were the only times they were allowed to eat directly from the carton. It felt like a forbidden act that Dad shouldn't be told about. It was our secret. It was fun. Then back to bed, dreaming about happiness.

Also, my sons and I had a ritual of going to the neighborhood library every Friday evening—even during summer breaks. We would each choose a book to check out and read. We'd discuss our reading experiences on Saturdays, a week later. More time spent together!

On the housekeeping front, in the early days, the weekends required house cleaning, laundry, and cooking for a couple of days to get a head start on the following week. I shopped for groceries during weeknights after the boys were in bed. At that time of night, I was able to get in and out of the store without wasting time. I always had a list, making the trip predictable and seamless. And quick. And as an added bonus, store employees were usually putting out fresh produce and restocking shelves. Everything I needed was freshly stocked and no waiting in long lines at checkout. The best of all worlds.

Then Sundays. My husband's day with the boys. My day to take care of myself, to replenish my soul through the serenity of quiet contemplation. To be able to start again tomorrow.

*****

Something that was extremely important to me was for my sons to know where and how I was raised. Every summer, they would visit my mother, their grandmother, who they worshipped. I wanted them to know and experience my humble roots. They were learning the same lessons I learned in that little house in that poor neighborhood from the same woman who taught me that you can go anywhere, do anything, if you study hard and always do your very best. And they should never forget how blessed they were.

*****

Nighttime is when I'd hear the small feet of one of my sons making their way down the long, dark hallway to our bedroom. I'd scoop up whichever little one it was and bring him into our bed. No monsters there. I still wasn't a good sleeper, and once awakened, I couldn't fall back to sleep easily; so I would do what I called "haunting the house." I'd check on the son who had stayed in his bed and retuck him in. I'd look out of the window at the darkened driveway and yard beyond, check locked doors that had already been checked before bedtime—every action reminiscent of everything I had to do all those years ago when my father was ill, and I was the oldest at home. I wrote notes in the journal I kept next to my bed. Notes for some of my best speeches were written in the darkened room during those times.

Once I confirmed everything was as it should be, I returned to bed, shifting the small frame of my son a little to the right to make room for me.

Everything finally felt familiar and comforting. Finally, I could sleep again. Right after I said my prayers again.

*****

I don't remember feeling especially exhausted during those years, although I must have been a lot of times. I just carried on because there simply was no other option. I don't know how other women, with similar obligations, coped with constantly shifting priorities and responsibilities. But for me, I am a better wife and mother when I am also an employee and an employer. My work fulfilled my desire for tangible accomplishments while allowing me to provide a better life for my family. It also spoke to my need to give back through customer service, training, and mentorships.

I'm grateful for the lesson I learned early in my career and in motherhood: I am the best version of myself when both sides of my soul are fed.

CHAPTER 21

Search me, O God, and know my heart:
try me, and know my thoughts.

—Psalm 139:23

1988–2006

It's that pause. That space between the question mark and the first word of the answer, which is fraught with tension. That's the place where truth lives. That split second that feels like forever.

*****

It's time for annual performance reviews. Everyone gets one no matter what their title is. As it should be. Just as I was required to perform those reviews and communicate clearly the good and bad, the strengths and weaknesses of my employees, so too did my boss have to do the same for me.

This was my first review with this man, this company. My new boss started the conversation with a tone I suspected—okay, I knew—wouldn't end with glowing words that indicated a job well done. I was sitting right in front of him, so I was aware of his tight expression, his hunched shoulders, elbows resting on the desk with hands clasped tightly in front of him.

I knew that look, that posture. I'd seen it in meetings when he received news he didn't like and wasn't prepared to accept. He was wearing his "no-nonsense managerial" face. He believed he was ready for a meeting he knew would be contentious. He was wrong. I was ready too.

Even though I had exceeded literally every metric I'd been given as my objectives, he seemed inclined to downplay those accomplishments during his opening comments. It was clear he hadn't reviewed the objectives *he* had established for me against my actual results.

Before he could continue, I interjected. I had a question I needed him to answer before we went any further. I needed him to specifically quantify his definition of "successful performance" for my role. I needed him to "see" the performance rather than the person behind that performance. Objectivity versus subjectivity was what I needed from him. So I asked, "What does successful performance in my role look like to you?" I needed him to articulate specifics—this was no time for generalities.

*****

There was that pause. He took his time to respond. I could tell he was actually thinking about my question. When he spoke, he enumerated everything he expected from that position. My position.

I said, "Why don't we look at each metric individually, and you can assess what my contributions really were."

That approach worked. From exceeding both sales and closing objectives to coming in under budget in all departments to drastically improved customer satisfaction scores, the numbers were all there. They could not be disputed, and he couldn't deny them. I had achieved more than he had asked, more than had been expected. The truth, something he should have already been aware of, finally revealed itself to him.

The performance review was over, and I never had to fight that particular battle again. Of course, I knew I would still have to prove myself every step of the way. Every day. That was fine with me. That had been my life, my entire life.

By the time I had learned to approach every interaction from an offensive position, I had already endured the "slings and arrows" of so many fractious encounters. Those confrontations helped me get stronger, more secure in my knowledge and contributions.

*****

I don't know how many times I've been asked the same questions throughout my thirty-year career, virtually the same words asked in various ways: "How did you handle being passed over for promotions that you were qualified for?" "Didn't it make you angry when unthinking or biased people refused to work with or for you?"

How was I supposed to answer them, especially when they were asked by people who looked nothing like me? Who hadn't had life experiences that were similar to mine? Who couldn't possibly understand?

Those very questions were absurd. How would I *not* take it personally when no one wanted to hear my ideas, my opinions, and give them credence simply because they came from me? Of course, it was maddening. But showing that emotion was never an option for me. As the only Black and female manager, I stood alone.

The truth is, of course I experienced things, heard things, that made me extremely uncomfortable. And yes, angry. But so what? Who do I complain to? There could be no shouting from the rooftops, "I'm mad as hell, and I'm not going to take it anymore!" Who's going to have the courage to change the order of things and do what's right? Certainly not the people who were displaying that bias or tone deafness. They're completely fine with their position and believe I should be too. And I learned that when you're standing alone in those circumstances, you don't have the luxury of showing your true feelings. The philosophy I had to adopt was, "Grin and bear it." Until I was in a position to change things. And I always knew I'd get there.

Maybe some thought I lacked bravery by not showing my emotions. I tended to keep my own counsel, which, to my mind, was the only way to keep safe my goals and intentions. Maybe I was just savvy enough to know how to keep my career moving forward.

Every lesson I'd learned throughout my career could be summed up in three words: Choose your battles. And I chose very carefully.

******

Diplomacy. That was a necessary component in every exchange I had. My strong beliefs, strongly held, could not, at least at that time, be strongly stated. I exercised restraint when my different point of view wouldn't negatively impact or change an outcome. And I fought for my beliefs when I felt they would be imperative to the successful completion of a task or project. Through that approach, I gained the respect of superiors and subordinates alike.

That approach gave me credibility so that when I did speak—even if what I said was at odds with superiors—my words were really listened to. Finally, I was heard. My listeners were no longer writing me and my ideas off before giving them a fair hearing.

Success followed. It was so interesting to me to see how "smart" everyone began to think I was once they started to really see me. Hear me. And then watch as the results I promised became reality.

I hadn't changed at all. Their view of me had. They had finally chosen to listen first and judge last.

CHAPTER 22

Hear, ye children, the instruction of a father,
and attend to know understanding.

—Proverbs 4:1

1956–1965

I was not my father's first daughter. I was his second with two sons in between. I thought my older sister was beautiful. She was always good at putting outfits together, and she seemed so sure of herself—confident in the knowledge that she was the apple of our father's eye. As his firstborn child, he doted on her, and she knew it. She took advantage of it. At the time, I didn't know if she disregarded the rules of the house or if there were no rules until she broke what would have been one.

My sister had what I wanted—our fathers' approbation. She took it for granted. I was given what was left. My father wanted the world for her. We certainly never had money for "extras," so we didn't ask for any. But for some reason, my father thought it would be a good idea for my sister to learn to play the piano. That probably felt like "refinement" to him. So somehow, he scraped together $50 to buy a secondhand or thirdhand upright piano. It was for my sister. He'd spoken to the daughter of a minister he knew who gave music lessons. Payment for those sessions would be through free yard work for his church by my father whenever needed.

As always, my sister had other plans. She had no intention of learning to play the piano. She had zero interest in the entire prospect and absolutely no time for weekly lessons. She was fifteen years old, and her world revolved around her friends and her four-years-old-

82

er-than-her boyfriend. She said those hurtful words disdainfully to my father without regard for the thought and love behind that gift that was hers alone, or for the sacrifice the rest of us had to make because of that purchase. The disappointment on my father's face was heart-wrenching. My sister never saw it, though. She had already turned away to contemplate her next adventure.

Well…that piano wasn't going to play itself, and "everybody" knew boys weren't supposed to indulge in things like that. So that task, like so many others, fell to me whether I wanted it or not. She'd said no. I wasn't asked. So I started taking piano lessons the following week. I was eight years old then. I was taught to never say "hate," but I despised that old piano on sight. Of course, I couldn't say that out loud. So I went. No complaints voiced.

*****

My sister's defiance always made everything harder for me as the next girl in line. I had to be extra "good" because she wasn't. Unfortunately, she got pregnant at fifteen, completely shattering our father. Disappointed, he seemed to decide that he wouldn't allow his heart to be broken like that again, so he seemed to completely ignore me. He never complimented me on anything I did. He never said much to me at all.

One time, when I sewed an Easter outfit for myself, without the benefit of a pattern, he told me the skirt was too tight. He told me I was "sorry" when something I cooked for the family wasn't up to his exacting standards, even while devouring the food on his plate. He barely noticed me unless I was doing something "wrong." I don't remember getting a hug from him. Ever.

*****

"Amazing grace, how sweet the sound, that saved a wretch like me." That's a line from one of my favorite hymns growing up, and it was always part of my piano repertoire. I was sixteen when I got my first paying job. In fact, I got two jobs at the same time. I was the pianist for choirs at my church two Sundays a month, as well as for a different church on the two remaining Sundays. I played piano for the young adults' and children's choirs at my church and for the seniors' choir at the other church. I was in eleventh grade by then, and the money I made paid for school supplies—taking that burden off my parents' shoulders. Those piano lessons were finally paying off.

My father had been a deacon in our church my entire life. But after his survival from that life-changing aneurysm and his heroic fight to recover, something changed in him. There seemed to be a new resolve toward a larger purpose in him. Suddenly, he declared his call to the ministry.

*****

The demands of my jobs being what they were, I had never heard my father preach. I was always at a different church on those occasions. And I was glad. For some reason I didn't understand and couldn't explain, I was afraid to hear my father's sermons. I was nervous for him. I didn't want him to fail. And if he somehow fell short and didn't engage the congregation sufficiently, I didn't want to feel that sense of disappointment in my father. I knew it would feel something like a tangible and irrevocable loss.

One Sunday, my father drove me to my second job at the other church. As I was playing the final song before the sermon, I saw my father step up to the pulpit and take his place as the visiting minister. What was he doing? Inside I was screaming, "Oh no! I don't want this to happen! Please, God, let him do well! Please!"

At first, my gaze was fixed on my hands, which were clasped tightly in my lap. I couldn't look at him. I didn't want to distract him. I didn't want to be there. But I couldn't leave because my ride was busy preaching, and I had no choice. I had to listen.

Slowly, I found myself looking at the crowded churchgoers and their reactions to my father's words. They were enthralled! I was surprised. I was elated! Daddy was doing so well. I don't remember his words; I wish I could. I do remember his face. He was transformed, transported, and he took all of us with him. His eloquent words—whatever they were, elicited responses from the congregation that sounded as if they were speaking as one body directly to God. My father led them there. And I went with them. With him, my father. Oh, how proud I was! I knew my father was a man of God, and I was already proud of his strength and character. But I didn't know how much prouder I would be when I truly recognized him as a servant of God.

Relief. Pride. I couldn't wait to tell him how much I enjoyed his sermon. I'd never told him of my silent doubts about his abilities as a minister. I don't even know why I had doubts. The smile he gave me for my small compliment told me everything I needed to know. My father loved me, and what I thought of him meant something more than I had ever imagined it would.

I didn't know it then, but that sermon would be his last. He died less than a month later. I will never forget his very last words. My mother and I were with him when he softly said, "Always remember, everything happens for a reason." I believed those words then, and I believe them to this day.

*****

Often, understanding comes slowly. And for me, it took a while—years in fact—before an important realization became clear to me. When it did, I felt like I'd experienced a blinding bolt of lightning, the loudest clap of thunder inside my head—the real truth about that old piano.

Looking back at that time in my life, I felt I was being punished for something my sister did or, in this case, didn't do. I had to learn how to play that piano, the bane of my existence at the time, because she wouldn't. But now, with the passage of time that forces us to grow into our true selves, I am confident of one thing: Although my father bought that piano for my sister, I've come to believe it was never really meant for her. It had been meant for me all along.

There were lessons about discipline, responsibility, tenacity, and creativity that, that old piano taught me. Lessons I've never forgotten.

And in the end, it gave me a connection with my father no one could have foreseen. That piano and all those lessons were the reasons we were together for his last sermon in that church, on that particular Sunday so long ago.

*****

You can call it fate or something else. I think of it as God's knowing hands guiding our lives, intervening when He knows what His children need. I wish I'd understood that sooner. I wish I had thanked my father.

Even if he didn't realize it at the time, my father, through that old piano, had given me exactly what I'd always craved: a connection to him and my desire to feel accomplished in his eyes. Because he had never heard me play piano before, the lack of a critique told me that he thought I had done a good job. Without saying anything, my father told me everything. And I'm proud of both of us.

I guess that old saying is true: "With age comes wisdom."

CHAPTER 23

The Lord will fight for you, you need only to be still.
—Exodus 14:14

1997

I was recruited for, and accepted, a new division president's position the same year my youngest son graduated from high school. Empty nesters now, it felt like a good time to make a move that would enhance my career. It also felt great to be chosen for such a big job, a huge opportunity. I would be in charge of all operations in Houston, the largest new homebuilding market in Texas. And as a special bonus, it was a chance to return to my home city and state.

I inherited 224 employees, 3 office buildings with long-term leases, and 3 completely different new homebuilding companies that needed to be merged into one large, cohesive, and functionally excellent entity. I didn't expect smooth sailing. I did, however, expect all issues regarding the entire acquisition to be resolved before my arrival.

But that wasn't the case. Time to problem-solve. Time to fix what was broken by my predecessors and new bosses.

*****

Problem one. None of those 224 people had any say in, or knowledge of, the consolidation. Three different companies had been acquired, each with its own identity and mission statements, company cultures, and management teams. Each company's employees thought they were better than the other two. None was as good as they thought. Otherwise, no need for me to be there. They would already be successful on their own without intervention from the new owner or from me.

The largest of the three companies was purchased out of their fourth bankruptcy. Interestingly, those employees were the most arrogant, the least interested in becoming part of the larger group, and had the most vice presidents—two for every discipline instead of the usual one per position. Clearly, someone had difficulty making hard decisions about who should be in charge. This meant more overhead, a complete waste of company assets, and a disservice to the one vice president who was better than the other in their discipline. And make no mistake, there's always one who's better than the other.

I remember asking the vice president of finance for that bankrupt company why they couldn't seem to make a profit, why they'd ended up declaring bankruptcy four times. Her response spoke to the complete lack of quality management at the highest levels. She said, "I don't know. We never made a business plan that assumed we would lose money. We just did." Time and time again? Great acquisition, new company.

Problem two. What do you do with three separate buildings, none of which is sufficient in size or location to become the headquarters for the newly created, much larger company? Leases had to be renegotiated with the ultimate goal of relinquishing all of them.

Even though I hadn't enjoyed my time in sales, I was pretty good at it. I made my case to each landlord to relieve us of those burdens. And it didn't hurt my efforts that the Houston commercial real estate market was strong. Once I pointed that fact out to those landlords, they were happy—even eager—to terminate our leases and re-lease their buildings at higher rates. Win-win.

Problem three and the most important of all. When I was hired for the division president's position, it was by the chief executive officer for the entire enterprise. Curiously, the man who would be my immediate supervisor, the regional director for Texas, wasn't consulted. So of course, I instantly became his nemesis—someone he felt he had to guard against in case I was brought on to eventually replace him. Perhaps he should have been more confident in his own abilities. Perhaps he knew exactly what his shortcomings were and hoped no one else had noticed.

Once on board, I was told by my regional director that one of the stipulations *he'd* made to the owner of two of the acquired companies was that *his* man would get the position of leading all three companies. This commitment had not been shared with, or sanctioned by, the CEO or the corporate senior vice president of human resources. That number two man wasn't aware of that decision and of course, neither was I.

Early in the transition, both of us were summoned to a meeting with the regional director. We weren't given a reason or an agenda. Once there, we were told of this managerial dilemma that he had created. The second-in-command guy was surprised. I was shocked. Where was this coming from? The regional director knew very well who was supposed to be in charge of the entire enterprise. Me. But I wasn't *his* choice.

This meeting was an attempt to try to change the dynamics of leadership for the entire acquisition. My new boss wanted someone of his choosing, not someone who had been chosen for him. Certainly not someone with the ability to speak directly to the CEO whenever I chose.

So there we were. The two of us sat across the table from the regional director—a white man who'd never run a division and a short Black woman who had run several successfully.

The surprised expression on my recently designated competitor's face said it all. He wasn't expecting this new development and seemed unsure of his ability to succeed. But of course, he would welcome the opportunity to try. Like me, he was interested in his own potential and career growth. To his credit, or maybe not, he sat quietly during the entire exchange between the regional director and me. I could tell my new boss believed he could bully me into relinquishing the position I was hired for. He was wrong. I had no problem defending my right to the position that was already mine.

My new boss hadn't expected pushback from me. When he could see that things weren't going the way he'd planned, he tried another tactic. He proposed splitting the duties of division president virtually in half with the disciplines of construction, purchasing, and land acquisition and development reporting to the "new man." Sales and marketing, finance, warranty, customer service, and human resources would report to me. In other words, two cooks in the same kitchen with two different philosophies, personalities, experiences, and visions.

This proposal was worse than the first! There would be no real focus, no clear direction. Confused employees would not know who was really in charge, especially when problems involved one disciple who reported to him and the other to me. Whose word would be final? Mixed messages would abound. Employee morale would be compromised, which would ultimately lead to dissatisfied customers and lost profitability. Most importantly, because I had held the position before and he had not, I knew the truth of being a division president of such a large and complex organization: Experience matters. It is everything.

Unfortunately for my new boss, he didn't know me. He hadn't spent time trying to learn more about me. If he had, he would have known, or at least come to realize, that I don't back down. I don't give up. I don't give in.

The meeting ended with my division president title still intact. The regional director left and flew back to his office. I immediately met one-on-one with the "loser" of that unnecessary and embarrassing match-up and told him of my vision for the three combined companies. Because he was familiar with two of them, I offered him an elevated position of senior vice president of operations. In this new role, he would become *my* number two man. He would report directly to me, enabling him to learn how to work with managers of every discipline without the burden of final decisions. Those belonged to me.

In the end, we learned how to work well together, and our collaboration proved to be extremely successful.

CHAPTER 24

Let not your heart be troubled, neither let it be afraid.
—John 14:27

1997

It was only six months into this new venture when the call came. The summons for me, my senior vice president of operations, vice president of sales and marketing, and chief financial officer to present ourselves at the corporate headquarters in California. The meeting was held in a large conference room with beautifully paneled walls—and a long, well-crafted oval table surrounded by comfortably cushioned leather chairs. There were eight of them, six already occupied by a senior officer of the corporation. For this meeting, two additional chairs have been pulled up to the table to accommodate me and my three vice presidents. For some reason unclear to me then, it seemed that no one in the corporate hierarchy wanted to miss this meeting. No one smiled a welcome. No one stood to shake our hands as we entered. No one spoke. So we sat. We waited.

My team and I didn't ask for this meeting, which was beginning to feel ominous, like an inquisition. It was the result of my new boss's request to the corporate management team. He believed I would perform poorly, embarrassing myself and my team, which would allow him to terminate me and hire his own "man" for the job. Once again, he didn't know me.

Our meeting was scheduled for eight o'clock in the morning on a Monday. And because my team and I had to fly to California from Houston, we had to leave on Sunday, which was Father's Day. I believe that timing was no accident. It was meant to interrupt the celebration of that important day for all of us who had children. It was meant to intimidate, to remind us that we were their employees only as long as they wished us to be.

I looked around the table at that august body: the chief executive officer, the chief operations officer, the chief financial officer, the senior vice president of human resources, the regional vice president who had oversight for all Texas divisions as well as several other states, and my boss, the regional director for Texas. Because they were already seated when my team and I arrived, we took our places in the remaining empty seats. I sat at the CEO's right hand. No one spoke until everyone was settled. I hadn't been told what this meeting was about, but I'd been in this business and this position long enough to guess and consequently, to be as prepared as I could be under the circumstances.

Then it began. The inquisition. Appropriately, the first to speak was the CEO. He had no notes. He spoke from already acquired knowledge about how operations were proceeding in the Houston division. My division. It wasn't a particularly impressive performance since he had access to financial reports from every division, every month. He could delve down to a specific community level if he chose. And apparently, he'd done just that. He proceeded to communicate his dissatisfaction with our performance in several communities he felt were underperforming. Once he completed his monologue, the next speaker, the COO, was free to express his views. Not surprisingly, they mirrored the comments already made by the CEO. As I had suspected, the communities they focused on were those that these very same managers had overpaid for during the acquisition of one of the three homebuilders—the one they'd bought out of bankruptcy. No one on my side of the table was surprised.

Next up was the regional VP, and on it went until it was my immediate boss's turn. I didn't expect, nor did I receive, any help from him. All of those senior managers had the same message. They were completely dissatisfied with the performance of those communities. Yes, we were making money, but not as much per home as they wanted. Apparently, they'd forgotten that *they* had originally projected an overall loss, not profit, for the three combined divisions' first year, primarily because of that bankrupt company's past performance. The piling on was relentless. It lasted until my boss, looking particularly pleased with himself, finished up the "dressing down."

$$*****$$

I knew what this meeting was really about. They were trying to mitigate their incompetence for the poor decisions they had made during the due diligence phase of the acquisition. They needed someone to blame. That someone was supposed to be me. *Not so fast, gentlemen.*

All the managers have finally spoken. And now, all eyes were on me. My people looked terrified. I think my senior VP was saying a silent prayer of thanks for *not* getting the division president position after all. During each senior manager's monologue, it was clear we had no allies here. After the CEO's comments, while each of the others were taking their turn berating us, I began a mantra in my head: "You don't get to fall apart." I repeated that phrase slowly eight times. My lucky number. I was ready.

I knew they expected me to be obsequious, to make excuses, cry, something. When I spoke, my voice was strong, and these were my words: "First, gentlemen, thank you for sharing your concerns with us. We share them as well. I've listened carefully to all of you, and I understand your frustration. However, respectfully, I've chosen not to address the issues and concerns you've all raised, and here's why. I realize that what will sound like a reason to me will sound like an excuse to you. So instead, let's discuss the game plans my team and I have already devised to move these communities forward to the profitability levels *we've* projected to meet by year-end."

To their surprise, I had handouts in my briefcase. Yes, experience matters. I went through each community discussing specifics regarding sales goals, personnel moves, and financials by subdivision and community—including those they hadn't mentioned. I didn't want any lingering questions or doubts. Some of those senior managers had to share their document with their neighbor. Who knew there'd be so many of them in attendance? And they certainly hadn't given me a heads-up.

With my part of the presentation completed, we took questions. All of which we had anticipated and had either an answer for or a game plan ready to implement. All we needed was time. We simply needed to get to year-end when all questions would be answered. All concerns resolved.

The meeting ended. We left, triumphant. All of those managers we left behind finally believed in my ability to do the job I had been hired to do. Even my boss who didn't want to be my boss. I didn't care. Time to get back to work.

*****

When the three companies were purchased, corporate management had projected a first year's *loss* of $1.6 million to shareholders. By year-end, we'd actually *made* $3.2 million and increased customer satisfaction by 30 percent, another important metric they didn't believe could be achieved.

By the end of year two, operating under the business plan I developed with my managers, instead of one that had been created for us, my team and I were able to exceed every metric: revenue and profitability goals grew by more than $8 million over projections coupled with decreases in overhead costs; 1,427 total homes were delivered against my original projection of 1,420 settlements; and an increase in customer satisfaction rating to over 80 percent—up from the original low of 22 percent at the inception of the three combined companies.

Renewed, intensive training and detailed cost control measures were integral to our growth into one cohesive entity working together toward one overall goal: accomplishing the mission we'd promised.

*****

Finally, even the company that was acquired out of bankruptcy was profitable. It's interesting what can be achieved through strategic planning, clear communication, and conscientious execution without the burden of mistakes and incorrect assumptions caused by poor due diligence during the acquisition phase in year one.

Enough said.

CHAPTER 25

*She is more precious than rubies: and all the things thou
canst desire are not to be compared unto her.*

—Proverbs 3:15

December 7, 2021

I'm tired—the kind of tired that sleep can't touch. It feels like there's cement in my bones, weighing me down. It's hard to breathe, too easy to cry. I recognize this feeling of devastation. I've felt it before. Too many times.

It's Tuesday, but not just any Tuesday. My baby sister died today.

*****

Growing up, she was the epitome of the word *carefree*. Her zest for life was evident in everything she did. While that same zeal was probably her greatest gift, it was also her greatest enemy. She possessed a desire and willingness to experience and explore every-thing—at least once.

Her childhood was like all of ours who grew up in that modest little house. She played in the front yard where grass had stopped growing years earlier. The packed dirt, a leftover from all the small feet playing in that yard over the years, was perfect for playing dodgeball and hopscotch. My little sister found her young girl pas-sion there—making "mud pies" flavored with the bold seasonings of youth: fearlessness, infinite time, and a sense of security from all things dangerous. She would indulge in her favorite pastime for hours. Of course, her dress was always stained and stiff from water and dirt mixed together for her prized "pies." She didn't care. She was happy.

Her given name was Elnora, after our grandmother, our father's mother. Without trying, she quickly earned a different name, and it suited her to perfection. We, her siblings and parents, called her Tiny because she was so little. The smallest of us with the biggest heart.

And she never slowed down. Movement was her superpower. I remember her constant motion and feeling exhausted on her behalf. But she just smiled when told to slow down before she wore herself out. It was as though, somehow, she knew her time on this earth wouldn't be long.

Smiles…always big smiles. A single dimple that appeared out of nowhere as if to highlight whatever she was thinking in that moment that we weren't allowed to share.

*****

"Bad things happen to good people." We've all heard that quote, but have we stopped to wonder why? For me, I've often wondered why certain people seem to attract more trouble, more heartache, more "bad things" than others. My sister didn't have a carefree life as she grew older. Was it poor decision-making, reckless behavior, or taking risky chances? Can it be that God gives extra doses of curiosity and the need to experience anything and everything, no matter the consequences, to those who choose a path no one else would dare? Maybe some are given extra strength to handle those hardships and hopefully get to the other side of their less-than-perfect decisions.

I don't know the answer. I don't even think knowing the answer is important. What is important is the fact that those flawed, magical individuals provide the rest of us with joy while they're here, even while we worry for their safety. We get to see lives that are lived to their fullest extent without regard for potential consequences. Turns out that can be both a blessing and a curse.

My sister made choices I never would have, took risks I would never dare. Her decisions led her down a path that forever changed her life, and ours. Experimentation with illicit substances was her kryptonite.

Crack. As the nursery rhyme goes, step on one and break your mother's back. Use crack and you will surely break your mother's heart. Crack was prevalent in almost every poor Black neighborhood back then. Apparently, it was relatively cheap and easy to access. There were no centers dedicated to understanding what crack addiction was or how to overcome it. She didn't get the medical advice she needed. It wasn't available to people like us. And we didn't know how to help her, to protect her. We did what we could, which was never enough.

As a close-knit family, we all stepped in to help her and her two children whenever called to that duty. Years passed, but eventually, she owned those actions and became better, stronger as a result. After her return to her "normal" self—freed from giving in to harmful temptations—we saw again her dedication to family, especially her two children, her fun-loving presence in the lives of all her nieces and nephews, and her unwavering pride in her only grandson.

And now, she's gone. The very thing that robbed us of our father years ago—that brain aneurysm—stole her from us years later. A genetic medical condition none of us had ever heard of until it became the nemesis of our family and changed our lives forever. Twice.

Aneurysm. It found her once and then again. She survived thirteen years after fighting the first one, and then she didn't. It struck her—struck us—again, and this time was the last time for her.

*****

Today is her funeral. It's raining. There's no way to ignore the sameness of this moment with that of my—our—father. It rained the day of my father's funeral, and it's raining now. Coincidence? I don't know. But it feels too familiar to ignore.

The sky is dark. The rain is drenching. It forces people to walk briskly under insufficient umbrellas, bent over like wizened old men. It feels like grief overflowing. Maybe it will stop soon…before everyone arrives.

Loss. It's experienced by each of us in our own horribly lonely and unique way. We each stand alone in that morass of overwhelming numbness and disbelief, even as the grief unites us. We experience it differently, but we all know that feeling when it visits us. You don't get over loss; you get through it…if you're one of the fortunate few.

*****

I keep asking myself how many times a heart can break before it simply stops completely, too broken to continue. It's an intriguing question without an answer. After losing both of my parents, two brothers, and now two sisters, unfortunately and painfully, death is no stranger to me. It's an unwanted guest who stops by when you're at your most vulnerable, when your back is turned dealing with other things that seemed so important only a moment ago. It never calls ahead to warn of its arrival. It makes its own timetable, unaware and uncaring of your plans, hopes, or dreams.

The residue it leaves behind appears without warning in the dark of night to wake you and torment you. And like a living nightmare, it never leaves, lingering stealthily, waiting to steal your breath without a moment's notice.

*****

Goodbyes like these always feel like forever. My hope, my prayer, is that it's not really forever—just a pause in time until we will all be together again. Whole, happy, free.

Goodbye for now, little sister. Rest.

CHAPTER 26

*I have shewed you all things, how that so labouring ye ought
to support the weak, and to remember the words of the Lord
Jesus, how he said, It is more blessed to give than to receive.*
—Acts 20:35

1984

He was like clockwork. A set-your-alarm kind of timeliness. Every year, about five days before Christmas, he would appear. Like an unwelcomed ghost of old man Scrooge himself. The Rent Man. Time to renegotiate an agreement that no one living had agreed to.

Being Black in the South back then, we couldn't count on much. But we could always depend on the Rent Man to show up to rattle my mother, to put overwhelming fear in her that she and her young children were about to become homeless. Unless she agreed to his new terms, of course.

*****

I'm finished with college now and working on my career. When I look back on those times, I remember my younger siblings playing outside, could hear him coming before his car actually stopped in front of our house. He drove a long, loud, two-toned brown and white, almost-new car. That car was imposing. He was not. He stood about five feet, five inches tall with a belly that pushed out precariously over his Texas-sized belt buckle and threatened-to-pop shirt buttons. Little kids are always told to be on the lookout for anything that could potentially put your eye out! And they were afraid those

101

poor buttons would lose their shaky grip and pop into someone's eye if the Rent Man got too close! As he approached the porch, they all seemed to move back a step as one unit, as though they'd rehearsed for hours perfecting this move and timing. And they always got the timing just right! It was actually comical to see.

He tried to appear nonchalant, but that demeanor deserted him the minute he stepped out of that car. Both hands were always in his pockets as if he feared he might be mugged at any moment by a little ol' Black lady and her band of small children. His small, too-close-together eyes darted around constantly as if he didn't want them to settle on anyone or anything too long. He was uncomfortable in our neighborhood where he owned several properties. He was afraid of his own "tenants." He was afraid of us.

By now, we'd learned that he was the real owner of our home. We all thought my mother and father owned the house with a mortgage that never seemed to get paid off. Apparently, that wasn't the case, or more to the point, wasn't the case any longer. During the last and most difficult time when my father was unable to work, with no money coming in and credit being something we didn't have, my father turned to this low-level loan shark wannabe.

I'm sure there were many "independent businessmen" like him operating in every neighborhood like ours. They were predators who took advantage of poor, ignorant-of-all-things-financial, "colored" folks who had no other options. I wondered how much of our neighborhood the Rent Man owned. Daddy had used our house as collateral for a loan he thought would carry us through that very difficult time until his health improved, when he would return to work, and pay off the loan. Then everything could go back to normal.

At least that was my father's plan. Of course, he hadn't expected to die so soon or so suddenly. He hadn't wanted my mother to worry, so he didn't burden her with knowledge of that transaction. Our mortgage payment had been replaced by a monthly rental amount of $25. That number doesn't sound large now, but when you don't have $25 a month, it might as well be a million dollars. And of course, it increased every year. The fear was very real. Every month. My mother never knew about this arrangement until the first time the

Rent Man showed up the month after my father's death. There was no warning, no opportunity for my mother to properly prepare for the debt she was about to inherit.

Somehow, without letting any of us know, my mother always found a way to pay that man. She didn't want *us* to worry.

When I could, I sent a little money home from my college jobs, hoping it would help out a bit. Later I learned that some of the few dollars I was able to send home went toward paying at least part of the rent for the home my mother and younger siblings still needed.

Mama never asked anyone for anything. Her favorite saying was, "God will make a way." And clearly, He did. Every month. We were ignorant of her situation. She was undaunted, or at least that's what we thought, because that's what she showed us. She had her faith, which was both her sword and her shield.

My mother. She was my first superhero, and she still is. She always accepted whatever life brought to her door. After all, to her, it was God's will, part of His plan for her life. And she had grit—a mama bear to all who belonged to her and to some who didn't. She had grace—that elusive "something" that carried her through everything effortlessly, or so it seemed to me. She was comfortable wherever she found herself. Relying on her faith to guide her. To be her true north.

*****

After college and at the start of my career, I vowed to take care of my mother's financial needs. And I did. Years later, once married, my husband, Ray, and I determined how much money we could afford to send her every month while still taking care of the needs of our small family. When I got a promotion and raise, so did my mother. Thankfully, I was doing well enough in my career for my mother to stop working at her babysitting job in the neighborhood nursery not too far from home. And she could finally breathe a little easier. I can only imagine how tired she must have felt, getting up early every morning to take care of other people's babies. Away from her own grandchildren.

When we could afford it, I decided to purchase my mother's home from the Rent Man, fulfilling the promise my younger brother, who died in college, no longer could. I wanted no more Christmas visits from her personal Scrooge raising the rent. Again.

*****

The Rent Man knew very well the true value of "his" property—that too-small house with too many people living there. A house that didn't even have an indoor bathroom until I was seven years old. The house was never insulated, and there was no central heating or cooling system, only a window fan in the living room and a big, open-faced gas heater in the small back hallway by the two bedrooms all of us kids shared—one for the boys and one for the girls. Dangerous, yes. Necessary, absolutely.

The Rent Man thought he could exploit Ray and me because he considered us to be ignorant of all things financial like he believed the other "coloreds" were who he dealt with. And because he knew we were doing this for my mother, he assumed that sentimentality would cloud our judgment and make us easy targets for overpricing that old house. He was wrong on both counts. Because of our work in the homebuilding industry, we knew the exact value of property in that poor neighborhood where there were no city amenities, like paved streets, sidewalks, or streetlights for children to stay safe. And so much more.

Ray and I met with him to negotiate a payoff amount. Once he pondered his options, a lump sum payoff immediately versus small monthly rent payments that we, on behalf of my mother, would challenge every year, he was eager to rid himself of this particular "asset." His offer was more than twice the assessed value. We offered him slightly half of his asking price. It was a fair offer, and the Rent Man knew it. He accepted that offer.

I'd lived in that house my entire life and knew the difference between assessed value and real, physical value. There wasn't much real value in our home or in the other homes in the neighborhood. Those houses were only valuable to those of us who had to live there.

We valued them because they were the only place we could afford. The only place we could call home. We settled on that figure even though it was much less than the Rent Man wanted, but one that was more in line with reality. Part of our agreement included the signing over of any and all rights he controlled regarding the land.

We didn't tell my mother about our intentions or our negotiations. In case we failed, I didn't want to disappoint her. It is now November, and I could tell she was already getting anxious about that year's upcoming Christmas visit. Failure was not an option.

*****

Mama's birthday was November 24 and usually fell on Thanksgiving. That year, my older sister, Rose, threw a combination Thanksgiving and birthday party for my mother. We were all there: siblings, in-laws, and children. Every family brought a dish or two. Sometimes three if you count dessert.

After our big Thanksgiving feast, it was time for Mama to open her birthday gifts; got to get that done before football games and turkey-induced naps. For the first time ever, there was no wrapped gift from me. Everyone was a little shocked. I had never missed giving my mother a birthday gift before. After all available gifts had been opened, shown around, and applauded, I told everyone that my gift wasn't there because it couldn't be wrapped. All eyes were on me now. What kind of gift couldn't be wrapped? Grinning as broadly as my face would allow, I announced that Ray and I had purchased our family home and would place it in an irrevocable trust for Mama. It was all hers for the rest of her life. No more Christmas visits from the dreaded Rent Man. No more anxious, sleepless nights for my mother.

Everyone's mouth, young and old, formed a big, round "O" with eyes equally wide open as the news sank in. Then, all at once, bedlam! There was jumping up and down, noisy exclamations of sheer, shared delight, hugging, laughing, crying, and praising God. And thanking me and Ray. What a great feeling for all of us! I looked around, and my mother was the only one still sitting. Her hands were held up to her face while she cried silent tears of joy and gratitude. We all crowded around her then, taking turns kneeling to hug her while quietly whispering affirming words of God's goodness and mercy.

*****

No matter the season or the occasion, my mother's favorite weekday attire was a dress called a muumuu, a word derived from the African Mandinka culture. It's a colorful dress that hangs loosely from shoulders to just below the knee. It was comfortable. It suited her personality—practical and no-nonsense. She wore them wherever she chose to go with no apologies given. In her mind, they weren't necessary. I have no memory of any other clothing she wore other than her Sunday "church" clothes. But not today.

Today is "Closing Day," and it arrived, clear and crisp and glorious. Odd weather for Texas during that winter season but somehow so very appropriate for this day. Ray picked my mother up and brought her to the settlement attorney's office. I left work and met them there. When I saw my mother, I felt such a rush of pride. She'd worn her very best Sunday church outfit—hat and all. Her broad smile and squared shoulders told anyone who noticed that she was a very proud woman on a mission, walking briskly and purposefully to an important meeting.

Head held high, clutching my hand, we entered the attorney's office together. Introductions all around. Papers were explained by the attorney and signed by each of us—Mama went first after a quick nod from me or Ray. She wanted to be sure she got everything just right. She couldn't stop grinning, and neither could I! She and I had been through so much together that had not been smile-worthy. Today's smiles and good wishes from the attorney were grateful rewards. Old wounds felt healed. Exhaustion miraculously disappeared. We all felt lighter—our spirits renewed. This must be what blessings feel like while you're actually receiving them!

My mother left home that morning as a renter. She returned as a homeowner—no mortgage payments, no more rent payments. No constant worry. She had just celebrated her sixty-fourth birthday, and finally, she owned her own home. She was still smiling as we walked out together; both of our eyes shining with barely contained tears.

*****

My mother gave the very best hugs, and I was on the receiving end of one of those before we parted. It felt like all her other hugs, warm and fully embraced. It felt like home to me. Her home now.

One of my favorite Bible verses is so true, "It is more blessed to give than to receive." Especially when the gift is for someone you love and who loves you back. Unconditionally and always.

CHAPTER 27

Be strong and courageous. Do not be afraid; do not be discouraged
for the Lord your God is with you wherever you go.

—Joshua 1:9

1981

It's Friday afternoon right before the end of the day and workweek for most people. Time for me to pick up files for each of the new homes my team and I will start first thing Monday morning.

I'm the construction manager for my community. I manage people and product. I also supervise the construction of several homes myself. Today one of the files I'm picking up is a house file for a new model home, which I will be responsible for constructing. There are already three models. But management has determined, based on customer demand, that a fourth, slightly smaller, nontraditional, family-oriented floor plan is needed. This model will have a basement and will be almost 2,500 square feet. Not very large, but large enough for a family of four. There are already families living in this relatively new community, and there will be many others soon.

I've driven to the Division Office to pick up all the paperwork I'll need for the construction of this home: purchase orders; standard and optional features chosen by the interior designer; exterior and interior color package information for brick, paint, and siding; and appliance selections. I already know which vendors and subcontractors I will use—we use them on most of our homes. They know our product, and they're good at their jobs.

As I'm leaving the office, house files tucked securely under my arm, my division president spots me and decides to give me a little "advice."

Without preamble, he says, "Cora, you know this is a new model. But we still need to sell houses on the weekends, so make sure you run a tight operation." I'm standing there wondering, when do I not run a tight ship?

He continues talking. "And don't, under any circumstances, leave a messy construction site. It still needs to look like an active model home complex."

"Yes, I know," I replied. I'm well aware of all of this since I'm in the community literally every day except some Sundays.

I turn to leave, again, and he starts to add yet another admonishment. I stop in my tracks. I've had a long and particularly difficult day because Fridays are always long and difficult—solving any lingering problems left over from the week, distributing payroll, wrapping up the week, and planning the schedules and priorities for the next week for both my contractors and team.

So before I even know what I'm doing, I turn around and interrupt him. I say, "You know, John, since you're clearly concerned about the mess I *might* make, why don't I simply build the model in five days! Then you won't have to worry about the weekend sales efforts."

His eyes speak volumes—telegraphing exactly what he's thinking about what I'd just said. And then, he says the words out loud… "As if you could." Really? Okay, gauntlet thrown. I've got to pick it up. Right now. And I did. I turn and leave, already planning the execution of this bizarre project.

*****

All of this is happening in Washington State, specifically Seattle, where it rains nine months out of the year. And we're not in one of the dry months, so I completely understand my division president's skepticism. He and I know exactly how long it typically takes to build a house—six months if we're lucky with the weather. Who wouldn't be skeptical? His words and attitude, though, galvanized me in a way that few others have before or since. And for some reason, I believe I can pull it off. I love a challenge, and this will certainly be a huge one.

Planning. It's everything. Always. But especially now. I drove straight back to the construction trailer in my community. The rule in our homebuilding company is the same countrywide. All new homes must start on Monday mornings. No exceptions.

There are ten major stages in constructing new homes, with lots of smaller steps in between. They start with forming the foundation or basement and end with walking the customer through their completed home, checking 244 items on our buyer's checklist. A house has lots of moving parts—more than five thousand—that must be checked, tested, and deemed to be complete and operational. Once the customer signs off, indicating their agreement that everything in the home is completed to their satisfaction, we can close, and they can move in.

Because my new construction home is a model, the "customer" who will perform the walk-through will be my immediate supervisor, the vice president of construction for the entire division. As with a regular, paying customer, the same 244-item walk-through checklist must be used.

And of course, I can't forget about all the independent inspections I'll need to get during the entire process. Unfortunately, county, city, and HOW (Homeowner's Warranty) inspectors only work from eight to five, so scheduling them within this process and time line is crucial. And I absolutely must pass each inspection the first time. There is no time for failed or second inspections.

*****

Now I need to assemble and talk to all the contractors I will need to get this insane project done. Thankfully, they're all still on-site, and rounding them up isn't difficult. They are just finishing up their workday too. I also must call each vendor to give them the same heads-up. They need to know, for example, that I will need my kitchen and bathroom cabinets delivered and installed at four o'clock in the morning.

Once everyone is assembled in the trailer, there's standing room only. Even my employees have decided to stay to find out what's so important. Every tradesman and subcontractor is wondering why they're here. Is there a problem so large that the distressing news must be shared with all of them at once? Surely, it is nothing good. I'm short, so I pull out a couple of pallets of paint supplies to be my makeshift stage. Complete quiet now. All eyes are trained on me.

My opening is all important. I begin, "Gentlemen, first, thank you for staying a little later today. I asked you all here because I have made a commitment that I can't accomplish without the hard work, expertise, and experience of each and every one of you." I have everyone's attention now, including my own employees.

"Together, we are going to make history. We're going to accomplish something that's never even been tried before in Washington State." Now they're virtually hanging on every word, wondering what I could be talking about.

I said, "Team, we're going to build a new model home in five days!" Audible gasps from everyone! "Yes, five days! I believe in the plan I've already developed. But most of all, I believe in you. All of you. So, what do you say? Are we going to do this?"

Almost immediately, stunned silence turns into uproarious outcries of "Yes, we can do it! We know we can. What's the plan, Cora?"

Deep sigh from me along with a big grin! "Okay, let's get started." Everyone settled down, started taking notes, and asking great questions. Every detail is discussed and planned out, especially the timing for each contractor to begin and end their part of the construction process.

It is unbelievably awe-inspiring to talk to everyone and see their initial reactions. They are all in—and enthusiastically so! Apparently, I'm not the only one who loves a challenge. None of us has ever done anything like this before. And undoubtedly never will again.

*****

Finally, it's midnight, officially Monday morning. I'm sitting in my car in front of the empty lot. It's dark, and I'm nervous, but I'm here. Ten minutes early. Since new construction can begin only on Monday mornings, my schedule for this project has to start one minute after midnight Sunday. It still feels like Sunday night to me.

Am I going to be the only one here until the contractors normally arrive? Did they forget? I'm sitting in my car in front of the empty lot contemplating calling this entire thing off. Just as I'm beginning to have serious doubts, to my delight and enormous pride in my crew, I look in my rearview mirror and see headlights coming my way. It's my concrete contractors leading two huge concrete trucks in. Every bit of worry and doubt vanished in that moment.

Time to execute the plan!

CHAPTER 28

Perhaps this is the moment for which you have been created.
—Esther 4:14

1981

I never expect perfection. I do expect your best effort. Always. My belief is, "If you say it, you own it." So I trust that promises made will be promises kept.

Commitments. I've gotten them from every contractor, vendor, and inspection agency before our insane, exhilarating five-day construction project began. Sequencing and timing are everything.

The beginning. Stage one. Metal forms are premade panels that are hooked together to define the perimeter, or footprint, of the entire house. Once they are all securely in place, they are checked by me and more importantly, the first county inspector who agreed to come in early to accommodate our schedule on his own time. He ensures that everything is in accordance with the blueprints. Now concrete can be poured. But before the pour can begin, I check the concrete company's paperwork to be sure the mixture of cement and additives are correct and accurate. This is a vital step that I was taught as a construction trainee. The mixture in these trucks is exactly right.

It's still dark. All vehicles on-site have their headlights turned on "high beam" and are facing the now giant hole in the ground surrounded by those metal panels. They are lighting the way for the concrete pour.

My concrete contractor has brought two teams of workers. This pour will go quickly. The teams are working diligently, smoothing the surface from the outside corners inward toward the center of the house to ensure a level floor. Before actual construction can begin, newly poured concrete must be "cured" to a PSI (pounds per square inch) of 2500—a process that normally takes several days of dry weather. We don't have time to allow the concrete to sit and cure naturally, and we are in a part of the country where dry days are few and far between. So "lime" has been added to the cement mixture to enhance and quicken the curing process—a practice that is common in areas high in humidity or rainfall.

In just a couple of hours, the framers can begin. Stage two. They, too, have brought two crews. I am so proud of these hardworking people. The mood is almost festive! As each contractor completes their tasks, they high-five the next crews entering the house—cheering them on. The entire framing process includes defining walls and reenforcing window and door locations as well as installing ceiling joists and roof trusses. Things are starting to take shape.

Next up, stage three, which includes the cornice contractors, roofers, and brick layers. They are responsible for installing siding, brick or stone, windows, exterior doors, and of course, the roofing material. Thankfully, no brick or stone was chosen for the exterior of this house.

Stage four. Time for the mechanical prewires and rough-ins. Enter electricians, plumbers, and HVAC (heating, ventilation and air-conditioning) contractors. All three teams will have to work in the house at the same time. Interestingly, they have already met as a group and mapped out a sort of "dance" to accommodate each step of their work: the plumbers will work in the kitchen while the electricians work in the bathrooms and bedrooms, and the HVAC guys start in the attic, installing vents and trunk lines. Then they shift rooms and spaces. And on it goes until every room has been touched and completed by all three contractors. What consummate professionals! Watching them work feels like poetry in motion to me. And I am so proud. If I had time, I might have wept from the sheer camaraderie of it all. But I don't, so a huge smile, handshakes, and pats on the back are all they get.

I am in the house as every stage begins and again when it ends—and a lot of times in between. Otherwise, I'm in the trailer on the phone with vendors to confirm arrival times for the materials my contractors will need for the rest of the construction. I am also calling the inspectors, again, to confirm the time they will be on-site. With everyone and everything confirmed, it's back to the construction site. I am never away for long.

By now, it's day two, and four of the ten stages have been completed, and the house is considered to be "dried in" meaning that work inside can be done without rain falling in, but the dampness remains. All three of the mechanical contractors complete last-minute items remaining from their initial installations. Insulation and drywall are next. Stage five. But before those tasks can be undertaken, I need another inspection. The first inspection was done immediately after the forms were set and before the actual concrete pour. That inspector was all business, and we passed with flying colors.

The second inspector arrives right on time. This inspection will determine, based on the blueprints, whether all doors and windows, electrical wiring, plumbing pipes, and HVAC trunk lines and vents are correctly placed. His sign-off indicates that everything that will be behind the walls is correct and can be covered with insulation and drywall. Once again, we passed. We knew we would because all of us—the responsible contractors and I—have checked and double-checked their work.

The morning of day three arrives, and it's time for drywall. I haven't left the construction site since I got here Monday morning, or Sunday night as I still think of it. Most nights I sleep sitting at my desk with my head on my folded arms. I wake up often to check the progress of my teams and deliveries of materials. A couple of nights, I sleep on the floor of one of my employees who lives in the community with her family. Thankfully, I'm able to use one of her showers every day. My husband brings me fresh clothes and toiletries first thing, for him, Monday morning. Unbelievably, the one thing I forgot to plan for was packing a bag for myself!

As has been the case every morning and throughout each day, contractors who have completed their tasks gather in the trailer to celebrate their achievements and to root on the next contractors who are starting their work. The momentum is high and contagious. Everyone feels it and is energized by it.

Except one. The drywall contractor. It's Wednesday, the third day. Very early Wednesday morning, or to my mind, really late Tuesday night, the entire area surrounding and including our community was hit with a major storm, bringing high winds and buckets of heavy rainfall. Unfortunately, nothing new in Washington State. The storm was fierce, but quickly over. Thankfully, the model home is dried-in, and work inside continued throughout the night uninterrupted.

Not surprisingly, it continues to rain throughout the rest of the day. Not drenching, but a constant drizzle left over from that huge storm the night before. The drywaller enters the trailer. He has made a decision. And with all the other contractors listening in, announces that he isn't sure he can get the drywall hung, taped, and floated correctly because he needs dry conditions in every room of the house. Even though siding, roofing, and windows are installed, there is no escaping the dampness inside the house and the trouble it could cause.

Before I can even open my mouth to respond, every contractor in the trailer starts talking to the drywaller all at once, saying, "There's no way you're not going to do your part! We did ours, and you need to do yours." They are serious and don't want to fail this challenge now that we're at the halfway mark. I am flabbergasted and extremely touched.

It's clear the drywaller can feel that small space between a rock and a hard place shrink with him standing squarely in the middle. The job of convincing him to continue our project is being done for me, which gives me a chance to come up with a plan. I interrupt the melee and thank all the other contractors for their support—some of whom haven't even done their part yet. I ask the drywaller, "What if we get construction heaters, one for each room, and have them blasting during the entirety of your installation. The painter can use them also, if necessary." To his credit, or maybe fear, the drywaller takes only a few seconds to consider my idea and quickly agrees. Everyone cheers, then scatters to retrieve enough heaters from other houses under construction while the drywaller and his crews stock drywall in each room of the new model.

Heaters are temporarily taken from other houses under construction and placed inside each room of the model. It takes hours, but finally the drywall is hung and completed. After my inspection of their work, the drywallers and I return to the trailer where everyone is waiting. I walk in first. My grin says it all. Applause erupts, and the drywaller and his crews are lauded like conquering heroes. Right then, my biggest cheerleader becomes the drywaller! He says to the painter, "Okay, I've left a great house for you. Time for you to get to work!" Loud laughter from everyone. What a release. What a relief.

Later that morning, well after the deluge of the storm has ended, my division president drives into the community and slowly passes the new model construction. His first visit. He doesn't stop. He doesn't come to the trailer where I happen to be observing his movements. Without stopping, he turns around and leaves the community. He speaks to no one.

Finally, it's Friday. The last day of construction. Stages six through nine of construction are completed on schedule—from all interior finishings to landscaping. No time has been lost even with that huge storm that ravished the area early Wednesday morning. Every contractor has done their part extremely well. Only one inspection remains—the final inspection that will signify that the house has been completed to the specifications of the county-approved blueprints. That inspection is scheduled for four thirty this afternoon, immediately after the completion of the landscaping.

We are all standing outside of the new home waiting for the final inspector from Homeowner Warranty (HOW) to arrive—me, my employees, and all the contractors. Spirits are extremely high. We know we've done what we promised, and the house is beautifully built and immaculate. We are proud of each other and ourselves.

The inspector's car turns into the community and stops in front of the new model. He asks for a copy of the county-approved master blueprints. I handed them over. He then asks who the superintendent is for this project. His question is anticipated because, at the final inspection, the superintendent responsible for the construction of the house is required to walk the house with the inspector in case he has questions or needs clarifications. As he asks the question, he's looking around at my employees and contractors. I step forward again. He looks at me as though he doesn't understand why I am even here, never mind being the leader of this entire group, this huge effort.

He looks me straight in the eyes and said, "I can't inspect this house."

No explanation was given, so I asked, "Why not? It's complete and ready for you."

His response is cruel, harsh. He said, "Because you're taking the food off the table of a white man."

I am stunned but manage to say, "My family needs to eat too." I doubt he hears me. He has already turned away, gotten in his car, and started to drive out of the community.

The silence he left behind is stark, naked, ugly. It's the kind of silence that leaves everyone uncomfortable—not knowing what to say or where to look. For what seems like forever, no one moves. No one speaks. I realize then that I have to act. I can't—won't—let all of our planning and hard, exemplary work fail. I immediately return to the trailer, call the HOW main office. I relay what has transpired with their inspector. I am given an apology, which sounds sincere. I don't care. What I want—need—in this moment is another HOW inspector dispatched immediately. And this time, one who will perform their job without bias. It takes almost two hours before our new model home is HOW-inspected. The inspector is thorough and takes a while, but we pass with no changes or questions.

No time to celebrate, though. I still need a signed-off 244-item checklist from my boss. The final house file will not be complete without it, and we will have failed to complete our mission. That walk-through is stage ten, and it is crucial.

No one has left the job site even though, by now, it is well past quitting time. Everyone is too excited to leave. We're all going to see this challenge through until the very end. What a great team! The local newspaper has somehow gotten wind of our efforts and was here earlier in the day with cameras to record and report on this historic event in their community.

*****

Time for my boss to inspect the house. Alone. As company protocol demands. Once again, I find myself waiting. At least I'm not alone—all of my guys are *still* here: employees and contractors. It is late by the time the walk-through ends, thanks to the hours delay caused be the HOW inspection issue.

Finally, my boss walks over to me and announces, "Cora, the house is very well done. Out of the two hundred forty-four items, I found only one that needs to be corrected, so I can't sign off."

What! I must have gone through that house with that very same checklist a hundred times at least—after every stage was complete and throughout the entire construction. I have no idea what I could have missed.

He tells me what the defect is, and I immediately remember that huge storm very early Wednesday morning. A large tree had fallen against an upstairs bedroom window. The tree was removed immediately, and the siding repairs completed. Apparently, though, it left a small crack in the far upper right corner of that window. I never saw it—I'm not quite tall enough. But that is no excuse. I asked my boss to wait. I will, somehow, get that window fixed before midnight! It is already close to ten o'clock. In the trailer, there is a book called the "Yellow Pages." I look for glass reglazers who are open twenty-four hours, and I actually find one! They come out almost immediately, fix the small crack—with me standing guard on a small ladder watching every move—hand me an invoice, and leave.

My boss inspects the repair and deems the house complete! He signs and dates the checklist and places it in the now complete house file.

My little army and I erupt into uproarious laughter, hugs, and congratulations. The biggest celebrant is the drywaller! We've done it! Together. And we feel victorious. It is just after eleven o'clock and finally time to go home. Time for bed.

I'll be back tomorrow morning to officially turn the keys over to the sales team.

*****

The following Monday morning, the division president drove into the community and came straight to the trailer. According to the salespeople, he toured the new model home Saturday afternoon and loved it.

He saw me and said, again without preamble, "I didn't think you could pull it off."

I simply responded, "I know."

He paused for a moment as though he wanted to say something more and then decided against it. He finally shook my hand, turned, and left. Nothing else needed to be said.

Mission accomplished!

CHAPTER 29

Blessed are the poor in spirit: for theirs is the kingdom of heaven.
—Matthew 5:3

Always

When you don't have much, what you do have means everything. Always striving for "more" while cherishing the little you do have. That was my life. Hand-me-down clothes were normal to me. As long as they were clean, no one else needed to know that I was not their first owner. Shoes with pieces of cardboard for soles didn't need to be discussed as long as you kept your feet on the ground. Solidly beneath you.

The saying, "Waste not, want not" could have been written specifically for my family when I was growing up. Lessons in frugality and restraint learned so long ago, during my formative years, still guide me to this day.

My mother. The smartest person I've ever known wasn't formally educated beyond the eighth grade. Maybe, because of that, she understood and respected the power of education. She bore eleven children—too many of those children leaving this earth long before they should have. She suffered through every loss and setback by relying on her unshakable faith and remarkable inner strength to get her through every pain and heartache.

She had no medical training, and there was no money for doctors' visits or medicines. So my mother made her own remedies guided by the potions she received as a little girl sitting at *her* mother's feet. She was confident in the knowledge she had gained. She kept us healthy with her common sense and homemade concoctions remembered from her youth. And we thrived.

There was no marriage, family, or therapeutic counseling. She simply dealt with whatever came her way. No complaints. One day at a time, one step at a time. She was courageous and a fierce protector. My mother was a true exemplar of the power of women.

*****

The power of women. Truly powerful women come in all shapes, sizes, colors, and cultures. They are fearless. They know how to take care of their business, their families, and themselves. I've been honored to know many powerful, talented women, and I stand in awe of their capacities to cope. To stay calm. To get things done. They don't give up, and they don't give in.

My sisters. All women of God who possess the same strength as our mother. They were and are strong, hardworking, courageous Black women. I am amazed by their unwavering sense of who they are, their dedication to family, and their strong commitment to God's teachings. They gracefully accept the blessings they received through their hard work, and they don't dwell on the challenges and obstacles placed in front of them every day. They are clear-eyed about the world and their place in it. Their beliefs are strongly held, and they don't mind sharing them. Their—our—philosophy is, "If you don't want to know what I think, don't ask for my opinion." Because the truth, as we believe it to be, will be the answer you'll get. Every time.

*****

Friendship. A word that has several meanings depending on whose experiences are being discussed. There have been so many incredible women whose paths I have been privileged to cross over the years.

When we're young, it's easy to make "friends" who you are absolutely positive will be in your life forever. While extremely rare, it does happen—to a very special few. As we age, and turn from youths in school, we approach that phase in life that I think of as the "great middle" of our lives. That time span when we enter adulthood with careers, marriages, and families of our own. The people we meet along those journeys feel like forever friends too. And some are. But one inevitable truth remains—some people are placed in our lives for a season; some for a lifetime. And as our lives are changing, so are the lives of those in our circle of friends.

That's the beauty of aging—being open to new experiences with new people who bring different perspectives and adventures into our lives.

Because nothing ever remains the same. Nor should it.

CHAPTER 30

Remember the words of the Lord Jesus, how He said,
"It is more blessed to give than to receive."

—Acts 20:35

2005

Oh, what a blessing! It was almost time for a gift I'd wanted to give my sisters for such a long time. The gift of travel and sisterhood togetherness.

I have five sisters—each one different and special in her own way. Age-wise, I am right in the middle with two older and three younger than me. All of my sisters are hardworking, strong women. They have raised their families and supported their husbands. Two of them have lost a son to violence. But they survived. Barely. They are women of faith, and their faith is unwavering even in their darkest of hours.

I have watched and learned from the older ones. I have taken care of and tried to be a role model for the younger ones. We treasured each other. We never questioned our love for each other even though I don't remember ever hearing any one of us say the words "I love you." It was simply understood, felt. We are our mother's daughters and followed the example she set without ever wondering if we should have chosen a different path.

My determination to give my sisters a memorable adventure was as much of a gift for me as it was for them. Not to show off, but to show my love for what I had been blessed to learn from them on my journey. After all, what good were the fruits of my labors if I couldn't, or wouldn't, share them with the women I cherished most? Women who couldn't manage it for themselves.

At that time, several had never flown in a plane. None had ever ventured outside of the United States. So my gift was an all-expense-paid trip to Paradise Island in the Bahamas. I made one concession to the all-girls group—my husband was allowed to tag along. Someone needed to keep track of our luggage! And he was very happy to oblige. Free trip for him!

The Plan: I purchased all the plane tickets, booked the hotel rooms, arranged for a limo to be at our disposal for the entire trip to take us on our sightseeing and shopping adventures, and I made reservations for meals. I wanted my sisters to know how deserving they were of some of the things none of them had ever experienced. I was obsessed with every aspect of planning this trip—making lists and checking items off as I accomplished them. I put together a "care package"—five in all—one for each sister, and FedExed that full box to one of my sisters. She was tasked with inviting the other four to her home in Houston where we could all be "together" by phone when each of them opened their individual package. I was almost giddy with anticipation waiting for that call. Once everyone was present, the call that I'd been anxiously waiting for came through.

Show and tell time! "Hi, ladies!" First, let's all thank Dee for hosting us."

Without asking, she had made a small dinner for all of them. A humble meal our mother used to make and one that we all still loved—"doctored-up" canned mackerel made into croquets and served with creamed corn. I know…not the best-sounding repast, but one that had been part of our childhood, and we loved it because it was always made by our mother with love.

"Okay, let's get started! Please open the package bearing your name. You'll find five different envelopes in each of your packages. First, take out the envelope marked 'Flight Information.' I had labeled each envelope to make it easy for all of us to experience each surprise at the same time.

"In this envelope you'll find your airplane tickets, both going and returning, along with your itinerary. Now, the next envelope is marked 'Hotel Information,' and these are your room assignments. You'll notice that all of you are on the same floor with connecting doors between each room. You can visit each other in your PJs without having to venture out into the hallway. We don't want to scare anyone!" Everyone laughed because, without a doubt, we all knew that our oldest sister would do just that without caring who saw her in her PJs and slippers.

"The next envelope contains your food vouchers. There are several wonderful restaurants in the hotel complex—from ones that serve breakfast buffets to all-day outdoor dining by the pools all the way to elegant dinner restaurants. Your vouchers will be honored in all of those restaurants no matter the day or time." *Oohs and aahs* all around now. We're talking about food—always a crowd pleaser in our family.

"The next envelope has a schedule for our tourist trips. We're going downtown to sightsee and shop, mingle with the local people, and take a ferry ride of the island. I've hired a limousine to take us from the hotel, wait for us, and bring us back when we're ready." There are squeals of laughter and actual applauding. These new experiences will stay with all of us forever.

"Last envelope, ladies. Please open them up." I waited, grinning but saying nothing. Just listening as all five of them ripped open their final envelope with unbridled anticipation. It didn't look like the others—just a plain, white, letter-sized envelope. This time there were no markings on the outside to indicate what was waiting for them inside.

All at once, I heard screams, hallelujahs, and shouts of "Thank you, Jesus"! I knew they were all standing and jumping and hugging each other. I didn't need to be there to know. Then a chorus of tearful "Thank you, Cora, thank you so much!" Of course, I was laughing and crying along with them.

Because I knew this trip meant taking time off from work, I wanted to give each of them a little money before they left to buy whatever they might need for the trip—from a new outfit to stocking their pantries and fridges at home for the families they were leaving behind. Inside each of those last envelopes were five crisp one-hundred-dollar bills.

Once they could hear me, I told them that, that money was just for them to buy whatever they needed for the trip or to pay bills they might not have enough money for once we returned. It didn't matter what they spent it on. It was theirs. I would take care of everything else once we were all together in Paradise. Happy tears that couldn't—wouldn't—be contained were being shed in Texas and Virginia all at the same time.

But perhaps the best gift I could give them—and the one they and I treasured most—was when I told them that there was one more gift. One they and I would never see. As it happens, Hurricane Katrina had just devastated Louisiana along with several other nearby states. I had already made a contribution to the rescue and recovery efforts of those courageous frontline workers and displaced citizens. My company at the time had committed to matching every employee's contribution, and I decided to split the matching contribution evenly and place them in the name of each of my sisters. End result, we were all part of "giving back" which, because of our upbringing, was more important than even the beautiful trip we were about to embark on. One they had been waiting to take their whole lives.

Interestingly, this news brought no screams, laughter, or applause. Only quiet tears of reverence and thanksgiving. We prayed then, led by my sister Dee. It was spontaneous and heartfelt. We gave thanks to God for His many blessings, for the sisterhood we were all part of, and for the values of giving back instilled in us by our mother and father so long ago.

*****

Our last evening in Paradise. We did everything on our agenda plus a lot more. Tonight, we dressed up for our final dinner. Just me and my sisters. We reconnected in a way that simply reaffirmed our unconditional devotion to each other. We retold old stories, laughed, cried, overeaten, tried new things we'll never have the opportunity to try again. And we felt blessed that we are all together on this journey called life.

As we waited to be seated at our table in a beautiful, five-star restaurant, there was a lull in the conversation…until my oldest sister quietly asked me a question. "Cora, how does it feel to be you?" It took me a moment to understand what she was actually asking me. I had no answer—I'm just me. But I believe I knew what she meant, and she was offering me the highest compliment she possibly could.

Without realizing it, through her question, my sister had given me a precious gift. And that gift was life-affirming for me. She thought I was special. I was extraordinarily humbled.

I still am and forever will be.

CHAPTER 31

So the last shall be first, and the first last for
many be called, but few are chosen.
—Matthew 20:16

1976–2006

Being first. What does it feel like to be the first person to invent something, to follow a path no one else has dared or dreamed of traveling? The first person to do anything? It feels lonely. I know.

There is no road map to follow. There is no one to call for advice or guidance. There is no conversation that begins with, "When you started your journey down your path, what did you do first? What did you experience? Where were the pitfalls? How did you overcome the obstacles you surely faced?"

Being first means you're completely on your own. And that's okay. It has to be because *you* are now the trailblazer in your chosen industry. And like it or not, you've got to figure things out on your own if you want to succeed. And you will succeed because that's simply who you are. You are not afraid to be first.

*****

My brother died in 1976. I lived in Connecticut then. That tragedy became the driving force to move my little family back to Texas where I grew up and where the rest of my family still lived. I secured a management position in the homebuilding industry where no one looked like me—either in gender or ethnicity. It was an industry I knew nothing about and had never explored. First hurdle,

I needed to find a way to take the mystery out of my being different from everyone else.

I learned immediately that expertise, once displayed and noticed, tended to mitigate any other "baggage" that might be attached to the person behind the performance. Excellence trumps everything else.

Focusing on the work is essential while striving to be excellent every day. Every task. Every time. No detail is too small, no challenge too difficult to attempt. Always moving forward with confidence even when you're not feeling particularly confident. Once a decision is made, execute it to the best of your ability. And if during the execution, flaws are revealed, evaluate your new reality and reassess your plan. And then you pivot.

No one ever said that the first approach is the only approach. It's simply the first. You can never be afraid to say, "I was wrong, but here is the new game plan." The challenge is always being willing to continually evaluate your plan from inception to completion and at every step along the way. Then refocus yourself and your team.

*****

"Jesus Christ doesn't walk among us. We are His imperfect creations who are doing the best we can." That was my message to all of my teams throughout my career. And to myself. That belief gave me the courage to never let setbacks become upsets. It allowed me to move forward in a different direction without feeling as though failure was inevitable. It was liberating in that way. It enabled me to feel secure in the knowledge that, should another obstacle arise, I—along with my team—would meet that challenge too. Head-on.

I'm well aware of my capabilities. But I am even more aware of my shortcomings. It is important to know who you are, but I believe that it's even more important to know who you are not. I am a strong, hardworking Black woman. I am not special. There are many of us, no matter our ethnicity, who show up every day with strength and tenacity. We persevere. We survive.

*****

Several years ago, I saw a movie called *Hidden Figures*, which featured three extraordinary women of color who were integral to the NASA program during its inception. After the movie ended, I realized that I was probably a little like those brave, intelligent, and unsung heroes. They were the first of their kind in an industry dominated by white men. Although my experiences were not nearly as impactful or important as their shared mission, I realized then that I, too, had been a pioneer woman of color in my industry all of those years ago. There were no others in senior management positions during my time who looked like me. I realized then that I had also been a "first."

That knowledge changed nothing. And everything. I am proud of my tenure in that unforgiving industry. I am blessed to have had the opportunities afforded me during those years to grow into my authentic self, piercing stereotypical labels and flawed assumptions.

I am proud that I was "first." And I rest secure in the knowledge that I will not be the last.

CHAPTER 32

She is clothed with strength and dignity; she can laugh at the days to come." "She opens her mouth with wisdom, and the teaching of kindness is on her tongue.
—Proverbs 31:25–26

1998 and 2005

I have always heralded my mother, my sisters, and my strong women friends. But there are two other accomplished women who are part of this fierce sisterhood. They are my daughters-in-law.

God did not give me daughters by blood. What I received instead are strong, beautiful women who chose my sons as their life partners. They chose to become part of my family, and I am forever grateful.

When I look at their serene faces, full of intelligence and strength, I feel blessed. I feel a strong familial bond that I know is biologically impossible, but it still feels true somehow. How can they both remind me of myself? We don't share blood, but we share so much more: unconditional love for our extraordinary family, unwavering loyalty, and an unparalleled work ethic.

They each chose careers that enrich others before themselves. And they have excelled. My oldest is a headmistress of a prestigious private preschool and is responsible for molding young minds through the teachers and administrators she manages.

The other holds a senior management position in a nonprofit organization dedicated to the certification of medical professionals to ensure their readiness for public service.

Their careers are important. They are fulfilling, and they are necessary. And both women rise to meet their particular challenges every day.

These beautiful women are driven. They are accomplished. They are compassionate. And they are my daughters as surely as if God had given them to me as babies.

I treasure them. I am proud to be their mother—in law and in life.

CHAPTER 33

Jesus saith unto her, I am the resurrection, and the life: he that believeth in me. Though he were dead, yet shall he live.

—John 11:25

Tomorrows

Life is noisy, messy. Facing so many painful and lonely, even scary moments in my life taught me lessons that only lived experiences can reveal. And I've finally lived long enough to appreciate the most important lesson of all. It is the solace and restorative power of exquisite silence.

Snow softly falling on spiky treetops in winter's cold, sleepy nights. Misty mornings with foggy opaqueness over still ponds. The flicker of a candle lit to remember someone special. A breath caught in mid-exhalation from seeing a long-lost loved one.

That stillness evokes a beautiful ballet without music—elegantly fluid movements executed flawlessly.

But there were also trying times. Those times allowed me to see, to understand and feel blessed for the moments that brought joy, love, and peace. And quiet.

I have so many experiences and life lessons for which I am particularly thankful. Moments like the smiles from the tiny faces of my sons, created by God and loaned to me for a time.

My mother's pride in me when she attended my college graduation and again when she became a homeowner for the first time so late in her life.

My then soon-to-be husband, smiling and waiting for me as he stood next to the minister who would make us one. He stands by me still.

Strong, spiritual parents who taught me that nothing is impossible if you believe in God and yourself with motives that are pure. And all of my sons' unwavering devotion to God and family.

Holding each of my four grandchildren as babies and watching those same children grow into strong, intelligent, and hardworking young adults.

Big, noisy family reunions where there was always laughter, storytelling, and almost too much food!

My career that was both challenging and fulfilling, and my pride in seeing people who worked with me reach their full potential—climbing higher than they thought they could.

And seeing God's grace in everything I've gone through to get to the other side of fear, loneliness, and pain. And grief.

*****

I've never had a mentor. But I have always had heroes and angels. And I treasure each one. I'm grateful for those courageous souls I've met along the way. They helped me, saved me when there was nothing in it for them. Time and time again. What they gave was priceless when they decided to become a champion in someone else's story. That instinctive call to action while others looked on helplessly or simply turned away.

I have always been very aware that I stand on the broad shoulders of my mother and father, along with all of my ancestors who've gone before me. They were the courageous ones, although I'm certain they never thought of themselves as such. They saw life as simply doing what was necessary to survive. What was expected. No complaints because no one was listening. I am grateful for their strength and tenacity. I am humbled by what must have been arduous and unbearable times filled with never-ending discrimination, confusion, and fear. But they endured. Every day. They kept going. That knowledge has kept me going. Every day. Their legacy of hard work, integrity, and intellectual curiosity have made me who I am today.

*****

It's raining again. It doesn't matter, though. I welcome it because it feels familiar—like an old friend who's come to visit for a while. It falls gently, like a veiled mist. It's the kind of rain that invites you to stand in it with arms opened wide as if receiving God's blessings, eyes closed and face turned up to the sky. It feels cool and cleansing, renewing. It feels like forgiveness and grace—reminiscent of a benediction. A gift, given and received.

*****

At the twilight of my life, when no more tomorrows remain—only yesterdays—I pray that all of those who loved me will remember me as someone who loved *them* completely and unconditionally. I hope that those who met me while on *their* personal journey, who considered me a sister, mother, and grandmother, wife, or friend will remember me as someone who was always there for them, rooting for their success, and who was always willing to help in any way I could.

*****

Perhaps they will say of me the words my youngest son wrote about me so many years ago: "She is generous and honest, funny and fun, smart and complex, yet as simple as her ponytail. She has an energy that makes people around her feel better about themselves and capable of almost anything."

*****

On that day, I hope I can say of myself, "I have fought a good fight, I have finished my course, I have kept the faith" (2 Timothy 4:7).

*****

And I pray that God will say to me, "Well done, good and faithful servant" (Matthew 25:23).

*****

Welcome home.

ABOUT THE AUTHOR

Cora Wiltshire spent more than thirty years in the homebuilding industry. She served in senior management positions for several large national and international companies.

As such, before penning *When the Rain Stops*, her time was spent writing shareholder reports and annual business plans. She was devoted to dealing with daily issues rather than reflecting on her past life as the middle child of eleven growing up in the segregated South.

This book tells the story of her journey.